PRIESTHOOD

Spencer W. Kimball

N. Eldon Tanner

Marion G. Romney

Ezra Taft Benson

Mark E. Petersen

Boyd K. Packer

Marvin J. Ashton

Bruce R. McConkie

L. Tom Perry

J. Thomas Fyans

M. Russell Ballard

Dean L. Larsen

Robert L. Simpson

Vaughn J. Featherstone

G. Homer Durham

Robert L. Backman

Victor L. Brown

PRIESTHOOD

Deseret Book Company
Salt Lake City, Utah
1981

©1981 Deseret Book Company
All rights reserved
Printed in the United States of America
First printing September 1981

Library of Congress Cataloging in Publication Data
Main entry under title:

Priesthood.

    Includes index.
    1. Melchizedek Priesthood (Mormon Church)—Addresses,
essays, lectures. 2. Aaronic Priesthood (Mormon Church)
—Addresses, essays, lectures. I. Kimball, Spencer W.,
1895-
BX8659.P74   262'.14933   81-5394
ISBN 0-87747-859-7   AACR2

CONTENTS

THE PRIVILEGE
OF HOLDING
THE PRIESTHOOD

President Spencer W. Kimball

My beloved brethren, it is a great privilege and blessing to hold the priesthood of God. Priesthood is divine authority bestowed upon worthy men that they might officiate in the ordinances of the gospel. The keys that have been given to those who hold the priesthood have come from heaven, for the priesthood is an everlasting principle that has existed with God from the beginning, and it will exist throughout all eternity.

Our fifth Article of Faith states: "We believe that a man must be called of God, by prophecy, and by the laying on of hands, by those who are in authority, to preach the Gospel and administer in the ordinances thereof."

Adam held that authority, as did others of the ancient prophets. The importance of the priesthood was expressed by father Abraham, who said:

". . . I sought for the blessings of the fathers, and the right whereunto I should be ordained to administer the same; having been myself a follower of righteousness, desiring also to be one who possessed great knowledge, and to be a greater follower of righteousness, and to possess a greater knowledge, and to be a father of many nations, a prince of peace, and desiring to receive instructions, and to keep the commandments of God, I became a rightful heir, a High Priest, holding the right belonging to the fathers." (Abraham 1:2.)

It was ten generations, I believe, from Adam to Noah, and then it was ten generations from Noah to Abraham. He inherited the blessings of the fathers. And who are the fathers? They were the righteous men who were the patriarchs to the nations in those first years. Abraham says:

"It was conferred upon me from the fathers; it came down from the fathers, from the beginning of time, yea, even from the beginning, or before the foundations of the earth to the

1

present time, even the right of the firstborn, on the first man, who is Adam, our first father, through the fathers unto me.

"I sought for mine appointment unto the Priesthood according to the appointment of God unto the fathers concerning the seed." (Abraham 1:3-4.)

This is something that we are heir to; we were born to it, and all we need to do is qualify for it to obtain this blessing, without which we could never go to the temple. And never going to the temple, we could never be sealed. And therefore, we could have no families; we could not go on with our work.

"My fathers having turned from their righteousness, and from the holy commandments which the Lord their God had given unto them, unto the worshiping of the gods of the heathen, utterly refused to hearken to my voice." (Abraham 1:5.)

When the wicked priests of Pharaoh tried to sacrifice Abraham on the altar, "behold, I lifted up my voice unto the Lord my God, and the Lord hearkened and heard, and he filled me with the vision of the Almighty, and the angel of his presence stood by me, and immediately unloosed my bands;

"And his voice was unto me: Abraham, Abraham, behold, my name is Jehovah, and I have heard thee, and have come down to deliver thee, and to take thee away from thy father's house, and from all thy kins-folk, into a strange land which thou knowest not of. . . .

"Behold, I will lead thee by my hand, and I will take thee, to put upon thee *my name*, even the Priesthood of thy father, and my power shall be over thee.

"As it was with Noah so shall it be with thee; but through thy ministry my name shall be known in the earth forever, for I am thy God." (Abraham 1:18-19. Italics added.)

"To put upon thee *my name*"! The name of Jesus Christ. The priesthood is called the "Holy Priesthood, after the Order of the Son of God." (D&C 107:3.) Melchizedek's name was given to the priesthood so we wouldn't repeat too often the name of the Son of God.

2

"I shall endeavor, hereafter," Abraham said, "to delineate the chronology running back from myself to the beginning of the creation, for the records have come into my hands, which I hold unto this present time. . . .

"But the records of the fathers, even the patriarchs, concerning the right of the Priesthood, the Lord my God preserved in mine own hands: therefore a knowledge of the beginning of the creation, and also of the planets, and of the stars, as they were made known unto the fathers, have I kept even unto this day, and I shall endeavor to write some of these things upon this record, for the benefit of my posterity that shall come after me." (Abraham 1:28, 31.)

Brethren, it is truly a blessing to hold the priesthood—to advance from deacon to teacher to priest—and then to hold that priesthood which is permanent, permanent as long as we are worthy of it, and which can be our shield and our way unto the eternal worlds. I pray the Lord will bless us that we may never consider it a common, ordinary thing to be "just an elder"—"He is only an elder." "He is only a seventy." "He is only a high priest." To be a high priest, *a high priest*, is really something in the life of any man. And to consider it less than unusual and wonderful would be to not understand the blessings that have been given.

I am a deacon. I am always proud that I am a deacon. When I see the apostles march up to the stand in a solemn assembly to bless the sacrament, and others of the General Authorities step up to the sacrament tables to get the bread and the water and humbly pass it to all the people in the assembly and then return their emptied receptacles, I am very proud that I am a deacon, and a teacher, and a priest.

In our special meetings in the temple, when the Brethren of the General Authorities come up to the sacrament table to bless, then pass, the sacrament, my heart beats more audibly again and I am grateful that I hold the sacred Aaronic Priesthood and have the privilege of taking care of the sacrament.

Then I remember that it was Jesus Christ himself who broke the bread and blessed it and passed it to his apostles, and I am proud that I can do likewise.

The Lord has given to all of us, as holders of the priesthood, certain of his authority, but we can only tap the powers of heaven on the basis of our personal righteousness. Thus, for the power of the priesthood to be truly felt in a family requires the righteousness of the men and young men therein. Our relationship with our wives, mothers, and sisters is one in which we kneel together, whether at the altars of the temple or in our own homes; we serve together, side by side, a beautiful partnership.

We are concerned, brethren, with the need to provide continually significant opportunities for our young men to stretch their souls in service. Young men do not usually become inactive in the Church because they are given too many significant things to do. No young man who has really witnessed for himself that the gospel works in the lives of people will walk away from his duties in the kingdom and leave them undone. We hope our bishoprics, who have a special stewardship in this regard, will see to it that they have effective quorum activities and active youth committees. As our young men learn quorum management, they are not only blessing other Aaronic Priesthood youth in those quorums, but they are also preparing themselves as future fathers and future leaders for the Melchizedek Priesthood quorums. They need experience in leadership, experience in service projects, experience in speaking, experience in conducting meetings, and experience in how to build proper relationships with young women.

We are rearing a royal generation, young people who have special things to do. We need to provide them with special experiences in studying the scriptures, in serving their neighbors, and in being contributing and loving members of their families. All of this requires, of course, time for planning and time to implement—anything but the casualness we sometimes see on the part of some fathers and adult leaders. We have reasons to believe that the impact of the world on our LDS youth is not only greater than it has ever been, but that it comes sooner than it has come in the past. Thus, we must do our work better and better!

We are concerned over the mounting number of divorces not only in our society, but in the Church. We are just as concerned with those whose families and marriages seem to be held together in "quiet desperation." Those who are careful and thoughtful in courtship will usually be careful and thoughtful in marriage. Those who thoughtfully enter the house of the Lord to be sealed for time and eternity are much less likely to experience divorce and difficulty, not only because of the influence of that sealing ceremony, but because usually they are better prepared for marriage in the first place. They have not only their love for each other, but a common bond of love for the gospel of Jesus Christ, which they knew before they knew each other. They also have some sense of the spirit of sacrifice and selflessness which underlies every happy marriage in countless ways.

We urge you as leaders, fathers, husbands, and sons—as holders of the priesthood of God—to develop even more your capacity to communicate with each other in your families, in your quorums, in your wards, and in your communities. Accept the reality that personal improvement on the part of each priesthood holder is expected by our Father in heaven. We should be growing and we should be developing constantly. If we do, others will sense the seriousness of our discipleship and can then more easily forgive us our frailties that we sometimes show in the way in which we lead and manage.

It is most appropriate for Aaronic Priesthood youth, as well as Melchizedek Priesthood men, to quietly, and with determination, set some serious personal goals in which they will seek to improve by selecting certain things that they will accomplish within a specified period of time. Even if the priesthood holders of our Heavenly Father are headed in the right direction, if they are men without momentum they will have too little influence. You are the leaven on which the world depends; you must use your powers to stop a drifting and aimless world.

We hope we can help our young men and young women to realize, even sooner than they do now, that they need to make certain decisions only once. We can push some things away from us once and have done with them. We can make a single decision about certain things that we will incorporate in our lives and then make them ours—without having to brood and redecide a hundred times what it is we will do and what we will not do. Indecision and discouragement are climates in which the adversary likes to function, for he can inflict so many casualties among mankind in those settings.

My beloved brethren in the priesthood, develop spiritual strength in yourselves, and there will be felicity in the family. Righteousness proceeds outward from the individual to the group. You will find that if you are converted (through studying, searching, and praying), your immediate desire will be to want to help others. True conversion causes us to want to reach out to the living and to the deceased to do what we can to help in each case. If we are truly converted, we will also want to provide for our own in the fulness of what welfare service means.

When the Savior said, "When thou art converted, strengthen thy brethren" (Luke 22:32), he was reminding us not only of an obligation we have, but also of the reality that we really can't strengthen our brethren much until we are personally strengthened.

No father, no son, no mother, no daughter should get so busy that he or she does not have time to study the scriptures and the words of modern prophets. None of us should get so busy that we crowd out contemplation and prayer. None of us should become so busy in our formal church assignments that there is no room left for quiet Christian service to our neighbors.

Brethren, it is a glorious privilege to have the priesthood of God, which has power that is greater than that held by kings and emperors. This is the work of the Lord. I know it, and I want you to know that I know it. The Lord has said, "I am the Almighty." "I am Jesus Christ." "I am Jehovah." He is the one we worship. We sing about him in our hymns. We talk about him in our meetings. We pray about him and through him in our prayers. We love him. We adore him. And we promise and rededicate ourselves that we will live nearer to him and to his promises and to the blessings he has given us.

As he was preparing to give up his mortal life on the

cross, Jesus met with his disciples and prayed: "This is life eternal, that they might know thee the only true God, and Jesus Christ, whom thou hast sent. I have glorified thee. . . . And now, O Father, glorify thou me with thine own self with the glory which I had with thee before the world was." (John 17:3-5.) May we also glorify our Lord and our Father through honoring and magnifying the holy priesthood that we hold!

SIX QUESTIONS
ABOUT
THE PRIESTHOOD

President N. Eldon Tanner

It is a great privilege, blessing, and responsibility to be a member of The Church of Jesus Christ of Latter-day Saints, where the priesthood and authority of God directs and administers the affairs of the Church. By and under this authority all ordinances of the Church are administered and received. It is even a greater privilege, blessing, and responsibility to hold this priesthood and authority, and it is about this divine power that I should like to write.

It would seem that this can best be done by answering questions that have been asked of me, such as:

1. What is the priesthood?
2. What is the basis for your claim that your church is the only one having the priesthood or authority from God?
3. Why do you claim that the priesthood is necessary in administering the affairs of the Church?
4. Who holds the priesthood?
5. What are the responsibilities of one who holds the priesthood?
6. What are the blessings of the priesthood?

What Is Priesthood?

Though I wish to deal with the priesthood as it pertains to the latter days, we must realize, as Brigham Young explained, that the priesthood is the law by which the worlds are, were, and will be brought into existence and peopled. It gives them their revolutions, their days, weeks, months, years, and seasons.

He further declared the priesthood to be "a perfect system of government, of laws and ordinances, by which we can be prepared to pass from one gate to another, and from one sentinel to another, until we go into the presence of our Father and God." (*Journal of Discourses* 2:139.)

The priesthood of God was delegated to Adam and passed on down to Abraham, who received it from the great high priest, Melchizedek, "Which priesthood continueth in the church of God in all generations, and is without beginning of days or end of years.

"And the Lord confirmed a priesthood also upon Aaron and his seed, throughout all their generations, which priesthood also continueth and abideth forever with the priesthood which is after the holiest order of God.

"And this greater priesthood administereth the gospel and holdeth the key of the mysteries of the kingdom, even the key of the knowledge of God.

"Therefore, in the ordinances thereof, the power of godliness is manifest.

"And without the ordinances thereof, and the authority of the priesthood, the power of godliness is not manifest unto men in the flesh." (D&C 84:17-21.)

Priesthood Authority

Now let us refer to the priesthood and its restoration in the latter days and answer the question of why we claim that our church is the only one having the priesthood or authority from God.

Our fifth Article of Faith states clearly: "We believe that a man must be called of God, by prophecy, and by the laying on of hands, by those who are in authority, to preach the Gospel and administer in the ordinances thereof."

This statement is in full agreement with that of Paul to the Hebrews. He said, in referring to priesthood ordinations: "And no man taketh this honour unto himself, but he that is called of God, as was Aaron." (Hebrews 5:4.)

One of the distinguishing and important features of the Church is its priesthood, defined so beautifully by President Joseph F. Smith: "[The priesthood] is nothing more nor less than the power of God delegated to man by which man can act in the earth for the salvation of the human family, in the name of the Father and the Son and the Holy Ghost, and act legitimately; not assuming that authority, nor borrowing it from generations that are dead and gone, but authority that has been given in this day in which we live by ministering angels and spirits from above, direct from the presence of Almighty God. . . ." (*Gospel Doctrine*, pp. 139-40.)

At the time Joseph Smith and Oliver Cowdery were translating the Book of Mormon, John the Baptist appeared to them. Announcing that he was acting under the direction of Peter, James, and John, the ancient apostles, who held the keys of the higher priesthood, he conferred the Aaronic Priesthood upon Joseph and Oliver in these words: "Upon you my fellow servants, in the name of Messiah I confer the Priesthood of Aaron, which holds the keys of the ministering of angels, and of the gospel of repentance, and of baptism by immersion for the remission of sins; and this shall never be taken again from the earth, until the sons of Levi do offer again an offering unto the Lord in righteousness." (D&C 13.)

Joseph Smith records that later Peter, James, and John ordained him and Oliver Cowdery to be apostles and especial witnesses of Jesus Christ to bear the keys of the ministry of his kingdom, and a dispensation of the gospel for the last times and for the fulness of times. (See D&C 27:12-13.)

At the time of the organization of The Church of Jesus Christ of Latter-day Saints, the Lord gave the following revelation to Joseph Smith: "Behold, there shall be a record kept among you; and in it thou shalt be called a seer, a translator, a prophet, an apostle of Jesus Christ, an elder of the church through the will of God the Father, and the grace of your Lord Jesus Christ, being inspired of the Holy Ghost to lay the foundation thereof, and to build it up unto the most holy faith." (D&C 21:1-2.)

The authority of the priesthood cannot be assumed or arrogated to oneself, but must be delegated by God through one having authority. One of the reasons for confusion in the churches today is that man has assumed this authority without proper delegation from the Lord. A man would have no more right to arrogate this priesthood authority unto himself than would one citizen or another decide to be a representative of the king or the parliament or the president of the United States. In fact, if one began to sign papers as their representative without having been properly appointed, he would be accused of forgery and handled by the law.

If the world could realize and accept this self-evident truth, it would not be difficult to agree that authority has been given or delegated by the Lord, as it was to Joseph Smith, to organize His church. But we must remember that whenever God places the true priesthood on the earth, there is always present a false priesthood, pretending the powers of the true priesthood. By faith and prayer and the witness of the Holy Spirit, we can distinguish the truth.

Why Is Priesthood Necessary?

We come now to the third question about the necessity of the priesthood in administering Church affairs. Only by the authority of the priesthood can the ordinances of the gospel be received or administered. Without it one cannot baptize, confirm, ordain, officiate, or hold any presiding office in the Church. In the women's organizations those holding positions as officers or teachers are called and set apart by priesthood authority.

In every dispensation of time there has been a leader who has held the priesthood of God. In this, the dispensation of the fulness of times, the priesthood has been restored and is now in The Church of Jesus Christ of Latter-day Saints, which is thus fully authorized to preach the gospel and administer the ordinances. It is evident that the source of the priesthood is the Godhead, and the priesthood held by man is delegated authority, without which delegation our labors would have no efficacy.

A further reason for the necessity of the priesthood is found in another Article of Faith, number nine, which states: "We believe all that God has revealed, all that He does now reveal, and we believe that He will yet reveal many great and important things pertaining to the Kingdom of God."

We know that God reveals his mind and will to his servants the prophets, and it is necessary for the Lord to have a priesthood representative through whom he can make known his mind and will and who can in turn serve as his mouthpiece to the members of the Church. Thus, it is necessary to have the priesthood in order to interpret and carry out the purposes of God.

Who Holds the Priesthood?

Our fourth question asks: Who holds the priesthood? We reply that any male who qualifies and is ordained may hold the priesthood and officiate in the office that he holds. However, there seems to be a tendency in the Church today to think that when a boy reaches the age of twelve he automatically is to be given the Aaronic Priesthood and be ordained a deacon, and that he should move forward according to his age in each of the offices in the priesthood, and then again when he is eighteen years of age that he should be ordained an elder automatically.

This is contrary to the teachings of the Church and to the order of the priesthood. Any man, young or old, in order to receive or be advanced in the priesthood should live according to the covenants he makes when he enters the waters of baptism and should be worthy in every way.

The priesthood is one of the greatest gifts and blessings a man can receive. Every parent, every teacher, every bishop, and every stake president should teach the applicant what the priesthood is, and the presiding authority should then satisfy himself by searching interview before the ordination that the young man is worthy in every way and that he appreciates what the priesthood means to him and what his obligations are. He must also be approved by the body of the priesthood.

Surely when God authorizes any man to speak or act in his name, whether he be a deacon, teacher, priest, elder, seventy, or high priest, he expects that man to be a worthy representative.

Imagine a young man eighteen years of age being given the authority to teach and baptize and ordain other young men as deacons, teachers, priests, and elders, with the same efficacy as those holding higher positions in the Church. Imagine what a great responsibility, privilege, and honor comes to him. Again we cannot overemphasize the importance of being worthy of this great blessing and of being an example to the world.

Priesthood Responsibilities and Blessings

Questions five and six deal with the responsibilities and blessings of the priesthood. One who holds the priesthood is to accept any office to which he may be called, or any assignment given by his presiding officer, to magnify his priesthood and to serve his fellowmen. Remember that the Lord said: "For whoso is faithful unto the obtaining these two priesthoods of which I have spoken, and the magnifying their calling, are sanctified by the Spirit unto the renewing of their bodies." And he follows with this great promise: " . . . therefore all that my Father hath shall be given unto him." (D&C 84:33, 38.) All is conditioned upon the magnifying of the priesthood.

We should all read, study, and understand the 84th and 107th sections of the Doctrine and Covenants, which deal with the priesthood.

I shall never forget the importance my father placed on the responsibilities of one holding the priesthood. Though we lived on a farm and were fully occupied, he emphasized that my priesthood duties came first. I was raised with the slogan and the belief that "if you seek first the kingdom of God and his righteousness, all other things for your good will be added unto you," which my experience and observation have proven to be right. My father also gave me opportunity in our home to function in my priesthood office and calling in blessing the sick, or other appropriate service.

One never knows what influence he may have on those with whom he is associated or how he will affect their lives. As priesthood holders, we must set an example of uprightness, be honest in all our dealings, avoid vulgarity and profanity, and demonstrate to our neighbors and all whom we meet that we live clean, honorable lives. *Keep the commandments.*

We should strive for peace and harmony in our homes and let this influence spread throughout the world. It is the responsibility of priesthood holders to maintain the standards of the Church fully and at all times encourage others to do the same. We must love our neighbors as ourselves and extend a helping hand to those in need.

The priesthood is for the blessing of all—men, women, and children. Through the priesthood we receive and administer the ordinances of the gospel, which include baptism, confirmation, the sacrament, and all temple ordinances, including sealings for time and all eternity, and work for the dead. By the power of the priesthood the sick are healed, the lame are made to walk, the blind to see, and the deaf to hear, according to their faith and the will of our Father in heaven. Blessings of the priesthood comfort those who mourn, and give aid to the stricken.

Indeed, if we were to understand the full force of what all this means, probably we would feel as Oliver Cowdery expressed himself in describing the appearance of John the Baptist to restore the Aaronic Priesthood and thus commence the establishment of the kingdom of God on the earth:

"On a sudden, as from the midst of eternity, the voice of the Redeemer spake peace to us, while the veil was parted and the angel of God came clothed with glory and delivered the anxiously looked for message, and the keys of the Gospel of repentance. What joy! what wonder! what amazement! While the world was racked and distracted—while millions were groping as the blind for the wall, and while all men were resting upon uncertainty, as a general mass, our eyes beheld —our ears heard. As in the 'blaze of day;' yes, more—above the glitter of the May sunbeam, which then shed its brilliancy over the face of nature! Then his voice, though mild, pierced to the center, and his words, 'I am thy fellow servant,' dispelled every fear. We listened, we gazed, we admired! 'Twas the voice of an angel from glory—'twas a message from the Most High, and as we heard we rejoiced, while His love enkindled upon our souls, and we were rapt in the vision of the Almighty! Where was room for doubt? No-

14

where; uncertainty had fled, doubt had sunk, no more to rise, while fiction and deception had fled forever!" (*History of the Church* 1:43.)

In a discussion of the priesthood, President J. Reuben Clark made this observation: If civil government of any of our communities were to be suddenly wiped out, the Church organization could govern the community if it were given the necessary civil sanction. He stated that the teachers, who are to keep the Church in order, could act as a police force. Bishops would be authorized to hold courts; high councils and presidents of stakes would hold other courts, both appellate and original jurisdiction, with an appeal to the presidency of the Church from a decision. Then he says that the authority resides in the President of the Church to make all necessary rules and regulations for the government of the people. It is clear that the organization of the priesthood is complete and perfect and is available and ready as and when the Lord comes to rule upon the earth.

An outstanding example of the perfect organization and power of the priesthood is the one explained by President Harold B. Lee regarding his experience when he was called in 1935 to organize the Church welfare program to turn the tide from government relief and put the Church in a position where it could care for its own needy people. He said that as he prayed fervently to the Lord for guidance as to the kind of organization that should be set up, he received the clear answer: "There is no new organization necessary to take care of the needs of this people. All that is necessary is to put the priesthood of God to work. There is nothing else you need as a substitute." This was done, and the welfare program has gone forward and is a monument to the power of the priesthood and is a model for the world.

Let us today each pledge our loyalty and devotion to the priesthood of God and follow the leader who is the mouthpiece of the Lord here upon the earth. As we do so we will not only contribute to the peace and happiness of ourselves and our families, but through service to our fellowmen we will be serving the Lord and preparing ourselves to dwell in his house forever.

THE COVENANT
OF THE
PRIESTHOOD

President Marion G. Romney

When we accept ordination to the priesthood, we covenant with the Lord that we will magnify our callings. At the same time, he covenants with us that if we do so, we shall be "sanctified by the Spirit unto the renewing of [our] bodies" and "become the sons of Moses and of Aaron and the seed of Abraham, and the church and kingdom, and the elect of God," and unto us shall be given all that the "Father hath." (See D&C 84:33-38.)

The specified penalty for breaking our covenant and "altogether [turning] therefrom" is that we "shall not have forgiveness of sins in this world nor in the world to come." (D&C 84:41.)

The Lord further said to the brethren assembled at the time he revealed the covenant, "And I now give unto you a commandment to beware concerning yourselves, to give diligent heed to the words of eternal life. For you shall live by every word that proceedeth forth from the mouth of God." (D&C 84:43-44.)

In order to magnify our callings in the priesthood, at least three things are necessary:

1. We must have a motivating *desire* to do so.
2. We must *search and ponder* the words of eternal life.
3. We must *pray.*

Desire

Over and over again the scriptures teach that men receive from the Lord according to their desires.

Alma declared: "I know that [God] granteth unto men according to their desire, whether it be unto death or unto life; yea, I know that he allotteth unto men, . . . according to their wills, whether they be unto salvation or unto destruction." (Alma 29:4.)

16

Jesus acted on this principle. In the translated version of the record made on parchment by John, the beloved apostle, we read: "The Lord said unto me: John, my beloved, what desirest thou? . . . And I said unto him: Lord, give unto me power over death, that I may live and bring souls unto thee. And the Lord said unto me: Verily, verily, I say unto thee, because thou desirest this thou shalt tarry until I come in my glory, and shalt prophesy before nations, kindreds, tongues and people." (D&C 7:1-3.)

At the opening of this last dispensation, the Lord said to the Prophet's father, "If ye have desires to serve God ye are called to the work." (D&C 4:3.) And two months later he said to Joseph Smith and Oliver Cowdery, "As you desire of me so it shall be unto you." (D&C 6:8.)

The importance of desire is dramatically pointed up in the following quotation from section 18 of the Doctrine and Covenants:

"And now, behold, there are others who are called to declare my gospel, both unto Gentile and unto Jew;

"Yea, even twelve; and the Twelve shall be my disciples, and they shall take upon them my name; and the Twelve are they who shall *desire* to take upon them my name with full purpose of heart.

"And if they *desire* to take upon them my name with full purpose of heart, they are called. . . .

"And now, behold, I give unto you, Oliver Cowdery, and also unto David Whitmer, that you shall search out the Twelve, who shall have the *desires* of which I have spoken;

"And by their *desires* and their works you shall know them." (D&C 18:26-28, 37-38. Italics added.)

The desire these men were to have was not a desire to be called to an office. Rather, it was a desire to take upon themselves the name of Christ "with full purpose of heart."

I remember one occasion in the mission field when I was trying to stir an interest in a discouraged missionary. I finally asked him, "Isn't there anything that you desire?" He said, "Yes, Brother Romney, I desire to be an apostle."

No one should seek to be appointed to any particular office in the Church. Such an aspiration is not a righteous

17

desire; it is a self-serving ambition. We should have a motivating desire to magnify our callings in the priesthood, whatever they may be. We should demonstrate that desire by living the gospel and diligently performing whatever service we are called upon to render. Holding a particular office in the Church will never save a person. One's salvation depends upon how well he discharges the duties of the service to which he is called.

The Prophet Joseph Smith said: "From a retrospect of the requirements of the servants of God to preach the Gospel, we find few qualified even to be Priests, and if a Priest understands his duty, his calling, and ministry, and preaches by the Holy Ghost, his enjoyment is as great as if he were one of the Presidency; and his services are necessary in the body, as are also those of Teachers and Deacons." (*Teachings of the Prophet Joseph Smith*, p. 112.)

Nor is an effective desire a mere wish. It is not impassive; it is a motivating conviction that moves one to action. One of the things it impels a priesthood bearer to do is to search and ponder the words of eternal life.

Search and Ponder

Since we cannot live by the words that proceed forth from the mouth of God unless we know what those words are, it is imperative that we study them. This the Lord has directed us to do.

As the Jews disputed with Jesus because he said that God was his Father, he pointedly responded: "Search the scriptures; for in them ye think ye have eternal life: and they are they which testify of me." (John 5:39.)

In the Lord's preface to his Book of Commandments, he said: "Search these commandments, for they are true and faithful, and the prophecies and promises which are in them shall all be fulfilled." (D&C 1:37.)

We are under divine instruction to "teach the principles of [the] gospel, which are in the Bible and the Book of Mormon." (D&C 42:12.) This we cannot do unless we know what they are.

To Joseph Smith the Prophet, Oliver Cowdery, and

18

John Whitmer, the Lord said: "Behold, I say unto you that you shall let your time be devoted to the studying of the scriptures." (D&C 26:1.)

To the Saints in Kirtland he said, concerning the instruction he had given them, "Hearken ye to these words. Behold, I am Jesus Christ, the Savior of the world. Treasure these things up in your hearts, and let the solemnities of eternity rest upon your minds." (D&C 43:34.)

As I have read the scriptures, I have been challenged by the word *ponder*, so frequently used in the Book of Mormon. The dictionary says that *ponder* means "to weigh mentally, think deeply about, deliberate, meditate." Moroni thus used the term as he closed his record: "Behold, I would exhort you that when ye shall read these things . . . that ye would remember how merciful the Lord hath been unto the children of men . . . and *ponder* it in your hearts." (Moroni 10:3. Italics added.)

Jesus said to the Nephites: "I perceive that ye are weak, that ye cannot understand all my words. . . . Therefore, go ye unto your homes, and ponder upon the things which I have said, and ask of the Father, in my name, that ye may understand." (3 Nephi 17:2-3.)

Pondering is, I believe, a form of prayer. It has, at least, been an approach to the Spirit of the Lord on many occasions. Nephi tells us of one such occasion:

"For it came to pass," he wrote, "after I had desired to know the things that my father had seen, and believing that the Lord was able to make them known unto me, as I sat pondering in mine heart I was caught away in the Spirit of the Lord, yea, into an exceeding high mountain. . . ." (1 Nephi 11:1.)

Then follows Nephi's account of the great vision he was given by the Spirit of the Lord, because he believed the words of his prophet father and had such a great desire to know more that he pondered and prayed about them.

President Joseph F. Smith tells us that "on the third of October, in the year nineteen hundred and eighteen, I sat in my room pondering over the scriptures. . . ." He had particular reference at this time to Peter's statement that Christ "went and preached unto the spirits in prison" (1 Peter 3:19) while his body lay in the grave.

"As I pondered over these things which are written," President Smith continued, "the eyes of my understanding were opened, and the Spirit of the Lord rested upon me, and I saw the hosts of the dead, both small and great." He then gives us an account of his great vision concerning missionary work among the spirits of the dead. (D&C 138:1, 11.)

Prayer

Desiring, searching, and pondering over the words of eternal life—all three of them together, as important as they are, would be inadequate without prayer.

Prayer is the catalyst with which we open the door to the Savior. "Behold," he says, "I stand at the door, and knock: if any man hear my voice, and open the door, I will come in to him, and will sup with him, and he with me." (Revelation 3:20.)

From the very beginning we have been instructed to pray. The Lord commanded Adam and Eve to "worship the Lord their God," and he later sent an angel to say to them, "Thou shalt repent and call upon God in the name of the Son forevermore." (Moses 5:5, 8.)

Jesus instructed the Nephites: "Behold, verily, verily, I say unto you, ye must watch and pray always lest ye enter into temptation; for Satan desireth to have you, that he may sift you as wheat. Therefore ye must always pray unto the Father in my name. . . . Pray in your families unto the Father, always in my name, that your wives and your children may be blessed." (3 Nephi 18:18-21.)

In this dispensation, even before the Church was organized, the Lord said to the Prophet: "Pray always, that you may come off conqueror; yea, that you may conquer Satan, and that you may escape the hands of the servants of Satan that do uphold his work." (D&C 10:5.)

He instructed the priests to "visit the house of each member, and exhort them to pray vocally and in secret." (D&C 20:47.)

Of Church members who went to build up Jackson

County, Missouri, he said, "He that observeth not his prayers before the Lord in the season thereof, let him be had in remembrance before the judge of my people." (D&C 68:33.)

And finally, he said, "Pray always lest that wicked one have power in you, and remove you out of your place." (D&C 93:49.)

In conclusion, I ask you to take note of Nephi's exhortation. I hope it moves you as deeply as it does me. He said:

"And now, behold, my beloved brethren, I suppose that ye ponder somewhat in your hearts concerning that which ye should do after ye have entered in by the way. But, behold, why do ye ponder these things in your hearts?

"Do ye not remember that I said unto you that after ye had received the Holy Ghost ye could speak with the tongue of angels? And now, how could ye speak with the tongue of angels save it were by the Holy Ghost?

"Angels speak by the power of the Holy Ghost; wherefore, they speak the words of Christ. Wherefore, I said unto you, feast upon the words of Christ; for behold, the words of Christ will tell you all things what ye should do.

"Wherefore, now after I have spoken these words, if ye cannot understand them it will be because ye ask not, neither do ye knock; wherefore, ye are not brought into the light, but must perish in the dark.

"For behold, again I say unto you that if ye will enter in by the way, and receive the Holy Ghost, it will show unto you all things what ye should do.

"Behold, this is the doctrine of Christ, and there will be no more doctrine given until after he shall manifest himself unto you in the flesh. And when he shall manifest himself unto you in the flesh, the things which he shall say unto you shall ye observe to do.

"And now I, Nephi, cannot say more; the Spirit stoppeth mine utterance, and I am left to mourn because of the unbelief, and the wickedness, and the ignorance, and the stiffneckedness of men; for they will not search knowledge, nor understand great knowledge, when it is given unto them in plainness, even as plain as word can be.

"And now, my beloved brethren, I perceive that ye ponder still in your hearts; and it grieveth me that I must speak concerning this thing. For if ye would hearken unto the Spirit which teacheth a man to pray ye would know that ye must pray; for the evil spirit teacheth not a man to pray, but teacheth him that he must not pray.

"But behold, I say unto you that ye must pray always, and not faint; that ye must not perform any thing unto the Lord save in the first place ye shall pray unto the Father in the name of Christ, that he will consecrate thy performance unto thee, that thy performance may be for the welfare of thy soul." (2 Nephi 32:1-9.)

May the Lord help each of us bearers of the holy priesthood to acquire such a powerful motivating desire that we will, through searching and pondering upon the words of eternal life and praying about them, be led to magnify our callings in the priesthood, and that we may thereby qualify ourselves to receive the promised blessings of the covenant of the priesthood.

THE KEYS
OF THE
PRIESTHOOD

Elder G. Homer Durham

The revised, unabridged 1959 edition of *Webster's International Dictionary of the English Language* numbers and lists twenty-nine distinct uses of the work *key* as a noun. As a transitive verb, four definitions are listed. The list for adjectival use is unnumbered and numerous. Among the nouns, usage number 24, a plural, is as follows: "*Mormon Ch. pl.* Power or jurisdiction of the presidency." Noun usage number 1 says "an instrument by which the bolt of a lock is . . . drawn. . . . The possession of the keys of a town, a building, or the like, . . . often made the symbol of authority." Number 2 states "that which affords or prevents entrance." Definition number 7 is "That which serves to reveal, discover, or solve something unknown or difficult." Number 8 adds "The mainstay; a leading individual or principle." All of these serve in one way or another to illustrate the role of the President of the Church, who holds the keys of the priesthood. He "serves to reveal" and is certainly a mainstay, a *key* man and leader.

As a transitive verb, the word has one set of usages that means "to fix, determine, secure, or regulate," such as musical pitch. Among the numerous adjectival uses are key industry, key radio station, key man or key woman in a group. Musically, adjectival use extends to key signatures, the sign (if in sharps or flats) after the clef to signify the "key" in which the music is to be played.

In all cases the word *key* or *keys* appears to indicate direction toward a more desired or meaningful condition or situation that, without "the keys," would be closed, or would have less or no meaning. The manuscripts of Mozart's delicate, graceful, sometimes emotionally charged music would be unintelligible without key signatures. Eliza R. Snow wrote of the "key of knowledge":

I had learned to call thee Father,
Through thy Spirit from on high;
But until the key of knowledge
Was restored, I knew not why.
—*Hymns,* no. 138

Few have explained the meaning of the keys of the priesthood better than President Joseph F. Smith, the sixth President of the Church. He stated: "The power of directing the Priesthood constitutes the *keys* of the Priesthood. In their fullness, these keys are held by only one person at a time, the prophet and president of The Church. He may delegate any portion of this power to another, in which case that person holds the keys of that particular labor. Thus, the president of a temple, the president of a stake, the bishop of a ward, the president of a mission, or the president of a quorum, each holds the keys of the labors performed in that particular body or locality." (*Improvement Era,* vol. 4, January 1901, p. 230.)

Commenting on this statement in 1936, President Joseph Fielding Smith, then chairman of the Melchizedek Priesthood Committee of the Quorum of the Twelve, wrote that "every man holding the Priesthood should understand that the keys of authority are centered in the president of the Church who is also president of the High Priesthood." Elder John A. Widtsoe described the use of a key in unlocking the door of a house, the ignition of an automobile, opening a safety deposit or jewel box. Without the keys there is no access, though we may own the property. "A man, likewise," he wrote, "holds the Priesthood . . . but can exercise its power, within the Church, only by the authority of the proper officials." (*Evidences and Reconciliations,* Bookcraft, 1960, p. 234.)

Ancient scripture contains references to the prophetic office such as that which is vested today in the President of the Church.

In reviewing the Old Testament, the Prophet Joseph Smith showed that in calling Moses, the Lord made known that he was his official representative. Recognizing the different roles of the two brothers Moses and Aaron, Moses was told: "And he [Aaron] shall be thy spokesman unto the people; and he shall be, even he shall be to thee instead of a mouth, and thou shalt be to him instead of God." (Joseph Smith Translation, Exodus 4:16.)

The Prophet Joseph, on October 5, 1840, told the Saints that Elijah "was the last prophet that held the keys of the Priesthood." (*History of the Church* 4:211.) In an address January 21, 1844, speaking of Malachi's prophecy of Elijah coming to "turn the heart of the fathers to the children, and the heart of the children to the fathers," the Prophet said the word *turn* should be translated *bind* or *seal*. The Saints, said the Prophet, may become saviors on Mount Zion by building temples, receiving for themselves and performing on behalf of their progenitors and others all the "ordinances . . . and sealing powers upon their heads." (HC 6:183-84.) Malachi declared that Elijah the prophet would be sent "before the coming of the great and dreadful day of the Lord [to] turn the heart of the fathers to the children, and the heart of the children to their fathers, lest I come and smite the earth with a curse." (Malachi 4:5-6.) The keys of the priesthood, with their binding and sealing power, thus have great meaning for the welfare of the human family.

During the Savior's transfiguration, Moses and Elijah appeared with him on the mount. Peter, James, and John were present and experienced this transcendent event. The Savior later instructed Peter at the coasts of Caesarea Philippi: "Whatsoever thou shalt bind on earth shall be bound in heaven: and whatsoever thou shalt loose on earth shall be loosed in heaven." (Matthew 16:19; see also Matthew 18:18.)

In over forty passages in the Doctrine and Covenants, the Lord clearly sets forth that the keys of the priesthood have been restored in this day. For example, section 65, verse 2, declares that "the keys of the kingdom of God have been committed unto man on the earth."

Section 81 specifies that the keys are held by the President of the High Priesthood. Referring specifically to the calling of the Prophet Joseph Smith, the Lord stated: "Unto whom I have given the keys of the kingdom, which belong always unto the Presidency of the High Priesthood: Therefore, verily I acknowledge him and will bless him." (D&C 81:2-3.)

Section 132, verse 7, declares that Joseph Smith, Jr., was appointed "to hold this power in the last days, and there is never but one on the earth at a time on whom this power and the keys of this priesthood are conferred."

In the same section we read: "For I have conferred upon you the keys and power of the priesthood, wherein I restore all things, and make known unto you all things in due time. And verily, verily, I say unto you, that whatsoever you seal on earth shall be sealed in heaven; and whatsoever you bind on earth, in my name and by my word, saith the Lord, it shall be eternally bound in the heavens; and whosesoever sins you remit on earth shall be remitted eternally in the heavens; and whosesoever sins you retain on earth shall be retained in heaven." (D&C 132:45-46.)

In a discourse May 12, 1844, the Prophet Joseph Smith, referring to this extensive scriptural record, stated: "All the testimony is that the Lord in the last days would commit the keys of the priesthood to a witness over all the people." (HC 6:364.)

President Joseph Fielding Smith recorded that in the winter of 1843-44, the Lord commanded the Prophet Joseph Smith "to confer upon the heads of the Twelve Apostles, every key, power, and principle, that the Lord has sealed upon his head. The Prophet declared that he knew not why, but the Lord commanded him to endow the Twelve with these keys and priesthood, and after it was done, he rejoiced very much, saying in substance, 'Now, if they kill me, you have all the keys and all the ordinances and you can confer them upon others, and the powers of Satan will not be able to tear down the kingdom as fast as you will be able to build it up, and upon your shoulders will the responsibility of leading this people rest.' "

President Smith continued: "Therefore, after the death of Joseph and Hyrum Smith, the Twelve assumed the authority of their office, the duty to preside over the Church.

Later, when through revelation the quorum of the First Presidency was reorganized with three presidents—Brigham Young and Counselors Heber C. Kimball and Willard Richards—they claimed, and rightfully, that since they were ordained under the hands of Joseph Smith, and from him had received all the keys and powers of the priesthood which the Prophet held, it would have been superfluous to have been ordained again. They were in this capacity, however, set apart and sustained by the unanimous vote of the saints, which was essential to make such ordination of force in the Church." (*Doctrines of Salvation*, Bookcraft, 1954, 1:259.)

President Smith demonstrated from the history of the Church that the keys and the priesthood were restored and always revealed to at least two witnesses. True, Joseph was alone in the Sacred Grove during the visitation from Moroni and when he first received the plates. But, "every time keys were restored," President Smith wrote, "two men received them. Why? Because it was necessary according to the divine law of witnesses for Joseph Smith to have a companion holding those keys; otherwise it would not have happened." (*Doctrines of Salvation* 1:211.)

Oliver and Joseph were both present when the Aaronic Priesthood was received from John the Baptist at Harmony, Pennsylvania, on May 15, 1829 (D&C 13), and when the Melchizedek Priesthood was conferred by Peter, James, and John in June 1829 (D&C 27:12-13). Both were present in the Kirtland Temple April 3, 1836, when Christ appeared and Moses, Elias, and Elijah appeared. Peter, James, and John were with Jesus on the Mount of Transfiguration. Peter's testimony of this event is eloquent:

"Yea, I think it meet, as long as I am in this tabernacle, to stir you up by putting you in remembrance;

"Knowing that shortly I must put off this my tabernacle, even as our Lord Jesus Christ hath shewed me.

"Moreover I will endeavour that ye may be able after my decease to have these things always in remembrance.

"For we have not followed cunningly devised fables, when we made known unto you the power and coming of our Lord Jesus Christ, but were eyewitnesses of his majesty.

"For he received from God the Father honour and glory, when there came such a voice to him from the excellent glory, This is my beloved Son, in whom I am well pleased.

"And this voice which came from heaven we heard, when we were with him in the holy mount.

"We have also a more sure word of prophecy; whereunto ye do well that ye take heed, as unto a light that shineth in a dark place, until the day dawn, and the day star arise in your hearts." (2 Peter 1:13-19.)

President Joseph Fielding Smith stated that if Joseph Smith alone had said "I testify, and I testify alone," the validity of his testimony could be challenged. Hence, there had to be two witnesses, "that the testimony might be valid." (*Doctrines of Salvation* 1:211.) Oliver Cowdery was ordained as assistant president by the Prophet on December 5, 1834. We believe that Oliver, with Joseph, received and shared in holding the keys. Oliver later lost his place, and it was taken by Hyrum Smith, as recorded in Doctrine and Covenants 124:94-96. Then the Prophet was inspired to confer every key, power, and principle the Lord had sealed upon his head upon the heads of the Twelve Apostles. Thus we see that the keys continue in the Church today, but governed by the principle that only one is authorized to *direct* the use of the keys, the President of the Church. The President is set apart in that position by the Twelve and sustained by the conferences of the Church.

The sacred temples of the Church are dedicated and their ordinances administered under the direction of the President who holds the keys at that time. Not only the ordinances of the house of the Lord, but all the ordinances of the Church are administered by men and women as they may be called by proper authority. Husbands and wives can be married for time and eternity and sealed as an eternal unit with their children by authority conferred and directed by him who holds the keys of the priesthood and who directs the work, aided by his counselors and the Twelve, each of whom have received the keys and can act in proper order upon the death of a President, and so on throughout the Church. The keys of the priesthood initiate and generate the influential services that, if respected and honored, can save the world from utter destruction.

The members of the First Presidency and the Council of the Twelve today have been given the powers to which we have been referring. But as President Joseph F. Smith said, *the power to direct* lies with the President of the Church. Said Joseph Fielding Smith, "The Twelve, therefore, in the setting apart of the President do not give him any additional priesthood, but *confirm* upon him that which he has *already* received; they *set him apart* to the office, which it is their right to do." (*Doctrines of Salvation* 3 (1956): 155.) Thus, calls, releases, and changes in assignments are carried forward in the Church, ranging from the ordinances of the temples to the blessing of babes, baptism by immersion for the remission of sins, the laying on of hands for the gift of the Holy Ghost, ordinations to priesthood offices, callings to preside over the Relief Society, Young Women, or Primary, or the calling and setting apart of men and women to various other offices.

The keys of the priesthood held and administered in turn by each president of the Church embrace and include authority to bind and loose on earth and to bind and loose in heaven. Their exercise on earth involves daily, but also eternal, consequences. The keys of the priesthood are keys to happiness. They derive from the Lord Jesus Christ, the Savior and Redeemer of mankind. All exercise and use of any keys delegated by the President of the Church stem from the Lord. Any and all use should reflect that source.

TEN BLESSINGS
OF THE
PRIESTHOOD

Elder Bruce R. McConkie

We are the servants of the
Lord, his agents, his representatives. We have been endowed with power from on high. We hold either the Aaronic
Priesthood, which is a preparatory, schooling order, or we
hold the Melchizedek Priesthood, which is the highest and
greatest power that the Lord gives to men on earth.

There are in this greater priesthood five offices or callings
—elder, seventy, high priest, patriarch, and apostle—yet
the priesthood is the same; and the priesthood is greater than
any of its offices. We are a kingdom of brethren, a congregation of equals, all of whom are entitled to receive all of the
blessings of the priesthood. There are no blessings reserved
for apostles that are not freely available to all the elders of the
kingdom; blessings come because of obedience and personal
righteousness, not because of administrative positions.

There are ten priesthood blessings that are available to
all of us who hold the holy Melchizedek Priesthood.

*Blessing one: We are members of the only true and living
Church upon the face of the whole earth, and we have received the
fulness of the everlasting gospel.*

"This greater priesthood administereth the gospel." It
"continueth in the church of God in all generations, and is
without beginning of days or end of years." (D&C 84:19,
17.)

The gospel is the plan of salvation; it is the way and the
means provided by the Father whereby his spirit children
have power to advance and progress and become like him.
The priesthood is the power and authority of God, delegated
to man on earth, to act in all things for the salvation of men.

Where the Melchizedek Priesthood is, there is the
Church and kingdom of God on earth; there is the gospel of

salvation; and where there is no Melchizedek Priesthood, there is no true Church, and no power that will save men in the kingdom of God.

Blessing two: We have received the gift of the Holy Ghost, and we are entitled to receive the gifts of the Spirit—those wondrous spiritual endowments which set us apart from the world and raise us above carnal things.

The gift of the Holy Ghost is the right to the constant companionship of that member of the Godhead based on faithfulness. It is the right to receive revelation, to see visions, to be in tune with the Infinite.

John, who held the Priesthood of Aaron, baptized with water for the remission of sins. Jesus, who was a high priest forever after the order of Melchizedek, baptized with the Holy Ghost and with fire.

The Holy Ghost is a revelator; he bears witness of the Father and the Son, those Holy Beings whom to know is eternal life. Thus it is that "this greater priesthood . . . holdeth the key of the mysteries of the kingdom, even the key of the knowledge of God." (D&C 84:19.)

The spiritual gifts are the signs that follow those who believe; they are the miracles and healings performed in the name of the Lord Jesus; they include marvelous outpourings of truth and light and revelation from God in heaven to man on earth.

Our revelations say that the Melchizedek Priesthood holds "the keys of all the spiritual blessings of the church," and that all those who hold this holy order "have the privilege of receiving the mysteries of the kingdom of heaven, to have the heavens opened unto them, to commune with the general assembly and church of the Firstborn, and to enjoy the communion and presence of God the Father, and Jesus the mediator of the new covenant." (D&C 107:18-19.)

Blessing three: We can be sanctified by the Spirit, have dross and evil burned out of us as though by fire, become clean and spotless, and be fit to dwell with gods and angels.

The Holy Ghost is the Sanctifier. Those who magnify their callings in the priesthood "are sanctified by the Spirit unto the renewing of their bodies." (D&C 84:33.) They are born again; they become new creatures of the Holy Ghost; they are alive in Christ.

Of such faithful persons among the ancients, Alma says: "They were called after this holy order"—that is, they held the Melchizedek Priesthood—"and were sanctified, and their garments were washed white through the blood of the Lamb. Now they, after being sanctified by the Holy Ghost, having their garments made white, being pure and spotless before God, could not look upon sin save it were with abhorrence; and there were many, exceeding great many, who were made pure and entered into the rest of the Lord their God." (Alma 13:11-12.)

Blessing four: We can stand in the place and stead of the Lord Jesus Christ in administering salvation to the children of men.

He preached the gospel; so can we. He spoke by the power of the Holy Ghost; so can we. He served as a missionary; so can we. He went about doing good; so can we. He performed the ordinances of salvation; so can we. He kept the commandments; so can we. He wrought miracles; such also is our privilege if we are true and faithful in all things.

We are his agents; we represent him; we are expected to do and say what he would do and say if he personally were ministering among men at this time.

Blessing five: We have power to become the sons of God, to be adopted into the family of the Lord Jesus Christ, to have him as our Father, to be one with him as he is one with his Father.

"Thou art after the order of him who was without beginning of days or end of years, from all eternity to all eternity," the Lord said to Adam. "Behold, thou art one in me, a son of God; and thus may all become my sons." (Moses 6:67-68.)

As the sons of God, we also have power to advance and progress until we become "joint-heirs with Christ," until we have "conformed to the image" of God's Son, as Paul expressed it. (Romans 8:17, 29.)

Blessing six: We can enter into the patriarchal order, the order of eternal marriage, the order which enables the family unit to continue everlastingly in celestial glory.

To gain the highest heaven and to enjoy the fulness of that light and glory which comprise eternal life, we must "enter into" that "order of the priesthood" which bears the name "the new and everlasting covenant of marriage." (D&C 131:2.)

Blessing seven: We have power to govern all things, both temporal and spiritual, the kingdoms of the world and the elements and storms and powers of the earth.

With reference to this, our scriptures say: "For God having sworn unto Enoch and unto his seed with an oath by himself; that every one being ordained after this order and calling should have power, by faith, to break mountains, to divide the seas, to dry up waters, to turn them out of their course;

"To put at defiance the armies of nations, to divide the earth, to break every band, to stand in the presence of God; to do all things according to his will, according to his command, subdue principalities and powers; and this by the will of the Son of God which was from before the foundation of the world." (Joseph Smith Translation, Genesis 14:30-31.)

Indeed, the Melchizedek Priesthood is the very power that Christ himself will use to govern the nations in that day when "the kingdoms of this world are become the kingdoms of our Lord, and of his Christ; and he shall reign for ever and ever." (Revelation 11:15.)

Blessing eight: We have power, through the priesthood, to gain eternal life, the greatest of all the gifts of God.

Eternal life is the name of the kind of life God lives. It consists, first, of the continuation of the family unit in eternity, and second, of an inheritance of the fulness of the glory of the Father.

All those who receive the Melchizedek Priesthood enter into a covenant with the Lord. Each such person solemnly promises:

I covenant to receive the priesthood; I covenant to magnify my calling in the priesthood; and I covenant to keep the commandments, to "live by every word that proceedeth forth from the mouth of God." (D&C 84:44.)

The Lord on his part covenants to give such faithful persons "all that my Father hath," which is eternal life in the kingdom of God. (D&C 84:38. See also 84:33-44.) Then the Lord, to show the binding nature of his promise, swears with an oath that the promised reward shall be obtained. This oath, as it pertained to the Son of God himself, is spoken of in these words: "The Lord hath sworn, and will not repent, Thou art a priest for ever after the order of Melchizedek." (Psalm 110:4.)

And with reference to all others who also receive the Melchizedek Priesthood, the scripture saith: "And all those who are ordained unto this priesthood are made like unto the Son of God, abiding a priest continually." (JST, Hebrews 7:3.) That is to say, they will be kings and priests forever; their priesthood will continue to all eternity; they will have eternal life.

"They are they who are the church of the Firstborn.

"They are they into whose hands the Father has given all things—

"They are they who are priests and kings, who have received of his fulness, and of his glory;

"And priests of the Most High, after the order of Melchizedek, which was after the order of Enoch, which was after the order of the Only Begotten Son.

"Wherefore, as it is written, they are gods, even the sons of God—

"Wherefore, all things are theirs, whether life or death, or things present, or things to come, all are theirs and they are Christ's, and Christ is God's." (D&C 76:54-59.)

Blessing nine: We have power to make our calling and election sure, so that while we yet dwell in mortality, having overcome the world and been true and faithful in all things, we shall be sealed up unto eternal life and have the unconditional promise of eternal life in the presence of Him whose we are.

Our revelations say: "The more sure word of prophecy means a man's knowing that he is sealed up unto eternal life, by revelation and the spirit of prophecy, through the power of the Holy Priesthood." (D&C 131:5.)

During the latter years of his ministry, in particular, the Prophet Joseph Smith pleaded fervently with the Saints to press forward in righteousness until they made their calling and election sure, until they heard the heavenly voice proclaim: "Son, thou shalt be exalted." (*Teachings of the Prophet Joseph Smith*, p. 150.) He himself became the pattern for all such attainment in this dispensation, when the voice from heaven said to him: "I am the Lord thy God, and will be with thee even unto the end of the world, and through all eternity; for verily I seal upon you your exaltation, and prepare a throne for you in the kingdom of my Father, with Abraham your father." (D&C 132:49.)

Blessing ten: We have the power—and it is our privilege—so to live that, becoming pure in heart, we shall see the face of God while we yet dwell as mortals in a world of sin and sorrow.

This is the crowning blessing of mortality. It is offered by that God who is no respecter of persons to all the faithful in his kingdom.

"Verily, thus saith the Lord: It shall come to pass that every soul who forsaketh his sins and cometh unto me, and calleth on my name, and obeyeth my voice, and keepeth my commandments, shall see my face and know that I am." (D&C 93:1.)

"And again, verily I say unto you that it is your privilege, and a promise I give unto you that have been ordained unto this ministry"—he is speaking now to those who hold the Melchizedek Priesthood—"that inasmuch as you strip yourselves from jealousies and fears, and humble yourselves before me, for ye are not sufficiently humble, the veil shall be rent and you shall see me and know that I am—not with the carnal neither natural mind, but with the spiritual.

"For no man has seen God at any time in the flesh, except quickened by the Spirit of God.

"Neither can any natural man abide the presence of God, neither after the carnal mind.

"Ye are not able to abide the presence of God now, neither the ministering of angels; wherefore, continue in patience until ye are perfected." (D&C 67:10-13.)

These, then, are *the ten blessings of the priesthood, the Holy Priesthood, after the order of the Son of God,* the priesthood that the saints in ancient days called after Melchizedek to

35

avoid the too frequent repetition of the name of Deity.

In this connection, these words from holy writ are appropriate:

"Now Melchizedek was a man of faith, who wrought righteousness; and when a child he feared God, and stopped the mouths of lions, and quenched the violence of fire.

"And thus, having been approved of God, he was ordained an high priest after the order of the covenant which God made with Enoch,

"It being after the order of the Son of God; which order came, not by man, nor the will of man; neither by father nor mother; neither by beginning of days nor end of years; but of God;

"And it was delivered unto men by the calling of his own voice, according to his own will, unto as many as believed on his name. . . .

"And now, Melchizedek was a priest of this order; therefore he obtained peace in Salem, and was called the Prince of peace.

"And his people wrought righteousness, and obtained heaven, and sought for the city of Enoch which God had before taken, separating it from the earth, having reserved it unto the latter days, or the end of the world;

"And hath said, and sworn with an oath, that the heavens and the earth should come together; and the sons of God should be tried so as by fire.

"And this Melchizedek, having thus established righteousness, was called the king of heaven by his people, or, in other words, the King of peace.

"And he lifted up his voice, and he blessed Abram. . . .

"And it came to pass, that God blessed Abram, and gave unto him riches, and honor, and lands for an everlasting possession; according to the covenant which he had made, and according to the blessing wherewith Melchizedek had blessed him." (JST, Genesis 14:26-29, 33-37, 40.)

This is the priesthood that we hold. It will bless us as it blessed Melchizedek and Abraham. The priesthood of Almighty God is here. The doctrines that we teach are true, and by obedience to them we can enjoy the words of eternal life here and now and be inheritors of immortal glory here-after.

I know, and you know, that as the heavens are above the earth, so are these truths of which we speak above all the ways of the world and all the honors which men can confer. God grant that we may keep the commandments and be inheritors of all that a gracious Lord promises his people.

APOSTLE AND PROPHET: DIVINE PRIESTHOOD CALLINGS

Elder Dean L. Larsen

The dictionary in our LDS edition of the Bible tells us that an apostle is "one sent forth." In this general sense the term has been applied to some who may not have received an ordination to the priesthood office of apostle. We even find occasional references to apostles of literature or science. This more general use of the term should not be confused with its application to an ordained office in the priesthood.

It is interesting that there are no references to apostles in the Old Testament. The first appearance of this office or title occurs with reference to the Savior's organization of a body of twelve, men whom he chose and ordained to the office. ". . . he called unto him his disciples: and of them he chose twelve, whom also he named apostles." (Luke 6:13.) To that group of twelve men he said, "Ye have not chosen me, but I have chosen you, and ordained you." (John 15:16.)

Although the New Testament record does not contain a wealth of specific information about the particular nature of the authority and responsibility associated with the apostles' ordination, there is enough to confirm that it had an overriding importance. To his newly ordained twelve the Savior said, " . . . whatsoever ye shall ask of the Father in my name, he may give it you." (John 15:16.) To Peter, the chief apostle, he said, "And I will give unto thee the keys of the kingdom of heaven: and whatsoever thou shalt bind on earth shall be bound in heaven: and whatsoever thou shalt loose on earth shall be loosed in heaven." (Matthew 16:19.) To the Twelve he gave this remarkable promise: "When the Son of man shall sit in the throne of his glory, ye also shall sit upon twelve thrones, judging the twelve tribes of Israel." (Matthew 19:28.) The universal scope of their responsibility was indicated in the Savior's charge to them: "Go ye therefore, and teach *all nations*, baptizing them in the name of the Father, and of the Son, and of the Holy Ghost: Teaching them to observe all things whatsoever I have commanded you: and, lo, I am with you alway, even unto the end of the world. Amen." (Matthew 28:19-20. Italics added.)

One of the special responsibilities of an apostle was disclosed in the selection and calling of Matthias to replace Judas Iscariot as a member of the Twelve. Peter explained to his fellow apostles on this occasion that the new apostle must "be ordained to be a witness with us of his resurrection." (Acts 1:22.) The charge to act as a special witness of the Savior is further developed in the modern scriptures, but it is clear from Peter's remarks on the above occasion that this was a sacred part of the apostles' calling in the earlier time as well. Peter made further reference to this obligation in his explanations to Cornelius and his family and friends when he said, "And we are witnesses of all things which he did. . . . Him God raised up the third day, and shewed him openly; Not to all the people, but unto witnesses chosen before of God, even to us, who did eat and drink with him after he rose from the dead." (Acts 10:39-41.)

Paul, in his epistle to the Ephesians, refers to the apostles as being the foundation of the kingdom of God, with the Savior himself as the chief cornerstone. (See Ephesians 2:19-20.)

Not only was the individual calling of each apostle one of great significance and responsibility, but the authority and responsibility assigned to the Twelve as a body or council was also very important in governing the Lord's people and his work. It is most significant to note the urgency of Peter and the other ten apostles to fill the vacancy in the Twelve left by the disaffection of Judas. This action occurred following a period of forty days during which the apostles received intensive instruction from the risen Lord regarding the establishment of his kingdom. (See Acts 1:3.) Two men, Barsabas Justus and Matthias, were apparently under consideration for this appointment, with the responsibility ultimately falling upon Matthias. (See Acts 1:23-26.)

It is possible that Paul and Barnabas, both of whom are

referred to later as apostles (see Acts 14:4, 14; Romans 1:1; 1 Corinthians 1:1; 9:5-6) filled subsequent vacancies in the council, although no conclusive evidence is given to this effect. We do know that other such vacancies occurred, as reported in Acts 12:1-2 regarding the martyrdom of James, the brother of John.

There can be no question from the New Testament record that the Council of Twelve Apostles directed the government of the Church following the death and ascension of the Savior. The role of Peter as chief among the apostles is also vividly clear. Nowhere is the policymaking, governing position of Peter and the Twelve better demonstrated than in the instance of reaching a decision as to whether the converted Gentiles, among whom Paul and his associates were having such great proselyting success, should be required to conform to the requirements of the Mosaic law in addition to their being baptized and confirmed. It is obvious that an intense division of opinion existed among lay leaders of the Church. Paul had pressed the issue because of his concern for his beloved gentile saints and the confusion that had arisen regarding their status. Consequently a leadership conference was convened in Jerusalem. "And the apostles and elders came together for to consider this matter." (Acts 15:6.)

After much disputation and discussion, Peter, the leader, proposed a policy for the Church to follow. This policy provided that the gentile converts need not comply with all the requirements of the law of Moses, but that they be faithful to their baptismal covenants, that they abstain from worshipping idols and engaging in practices related to their earlier religious beliefs, and that they keep themselves virtuous and pure in their personal lives. (See Acts 15:7-31.) Peter's proposal was sustained by the apostles and other leaders who had engaged in the discussions, and it became the policy of the Church.

This somewhat detailed account provided by Luke gives a revealing insight into the operations of the Church's governing council in the meridian of time.

It is important at this point to comment on the term *prophet* as it applied to the office and calling of an apostle.

While the Old Testament identifies many prophets, it makes no reference to apostles. The Old Testament prophets acted as authorized spokesmen for the Lord. They taught the true nature of God and declared God's will with respect to men and their conduct. Generally these specially called men served as official record keepers. They promoted faithfulness and obedience among the people and foretold the consequences of men's acceptance or rejection of God's will. They were leaders in the government of the Lord's work. The record gives ample testimony to the effect that these men were called of God. None of them was self-appointed. Moses had his experience at the burning bush. Joshua was told by the voice of the Lord: "Moses my servant is dead; now therefore arise, go over this Jordan, thou, and all this people. . . . as I was with Moses, so I will be with thee: I will not fail thee, nor forsake thee." (Joshua 1:2, 5.) Jeremiah was told: "Before I formed thee in the belly I knew thee; and before thou camest forth out of the womb I sanctified thee, and I ordained thee a prophet unto the nations." (Jeremiah 1:5.)

The apostles who were called by the Savior during his earthly ministry received the prophetic mantle as well. Throughout the New Testament record the terms *apostle* and *prophet* are applied to the same office. Paul speaks of apostles and prophets being the foundation of the Lord's church and kingdom. (See Ephesians 2:20.) He also declared that the word of God "is now revealed unto his holy apostles and prophets." (Ephesians 3:5.) Luke records the Savior's personal promise to "send them prophets and apostles." (Luke 11:49.)

As the Lord organized his church on the American continent among the Nephite people, he once again chose twelve men to give leadership to the work. (See 3 Nephi 12:1-2.) Interestingly these men are regularly referred to as disciples rather than as apostles. It is clear from the nature of the responsibility and authority assigned to them by the Savior, however, that they carried the apostolic ministry among the people of their time.

The Book of Mormon account adds verification to the fact that whenever the Lord's authorized church and government are to be found upon the earth in the period following his mortal ministry, apostles and prophets will serve as the central leadership. It is one of the identifying marks of the true church of Jesus Christ. It is true of his church today as it was in earlier times.

The preceding is perhaps adequate to establish the historic authenticity of the office and calling of apostles in those times prior to the restoration of the Lord's church and kingdom in the nineteenth century A.D. Because of this most compelling precedent, one who seeks for the true church of Jesus Christ among all of the religions of the present day might reasonably initiate that quest by asking which of these organizations is built upon the foundation of apostles and prophets. Certainly this identifying feature will be prominent in the true church today.

The calling and ordination of the first Council of Twelve Apostles in this last dispensation of the gospel to the earth is of sufficient consequence to merit some detail of description.

All of the keys, authority, and sealing powers conferred upon Peter and the original Twelve by the Savior himself were restored to the earth in the spring of 1829 as Peter, James, and John returned as heavenly messengers and transmitted these same keys and powers to Joseph Smith. The Lord alludes to this event in a revelation given in August 1830, when he said to Joseph Smith, "And also with Peter, and James, and John, whom I have sent unto you, by whom I have ordained you and confirmed you to be apostles, and especial witnesses of my name, and bear the keys of your ministry and of the same things which I revealed unto them." (D&C 27:12.)

On February 14, 1835, Joseph Smith assembled all of the men who had been a part of Zion's Camp. (For an account of Zion's Camp, see *History of the Church* 2:61-83.) He explained the purpose of this meeting to Joseph and Brigham Young:

"On the Sabbath previous to the 14th of February, (February 8th) Brothers Joseph and Brigham Young came to my house after meeting, and sang for me; the Spirit of the Lord was poured out upon us, and I told them I wanted to see those brethren together, who went up to Zion in the camp, the previous summer, for I had a blessing for them." (HC 2:180-81.)

The minutes of the meeting of Zion's Camp on February 14, 1835, give the following:

"*Kirtland, February 14, 1835.*—This day, a meeting was called of those who journeyed last season to Zion for the purpose of laying the foundation of its redemption, together with as many other of the brethren and sisters as were disposed to attend.

"President Joseph Smith, Jun., presiding, read the 15th chapter of John, and said: Let us endeavor to solemnize our minds that we may receive a blessing, by calling on the Lord. After an appropriate and affecting prayer, the brethren who went to Zion [in Zion's camp] were requested to take their seats together in a part of the house by themselves.

"President Smith then stated that the meeting had been called, because God had commanded it; and it was made known to him by vision and by the Holy Spirit. He then gave a relation of some of the circumstances attending us while journeying to Zion—our trials, sufferings; and said God had not designed all this for nothing, but He had it in remembrance yet; and it was the will of God that those who went to Zion, with a determination to lay down their lives, if necessary, should be ordained to the ministry, and go forth to prune the vineyard for the last time. . . .

"The President also said many things; such as the weak things, even the smallest and weakest among us, shall be powerful and mighty, and great things shall be accomplished by you from this hour; and you shall begin to feel the whisperings of the Spirit of God; and the work of God shall begin to break forth from this time; and you shall be endowed with power from on high.

"President then called up all those who went to Zion, if they were agreed with him in the statement which he had made, to arise; and they all arose and stood upon their feet.

"He then called upon the remainder of the congregation, to know if they also sanctioned the move, and they all raised their right hand. . . .

"President Joseph Smith, Jun., after making many remarks on the subject of choosing the Twelve, wanted an expression from the brethren, if they would be satisfied to have the Spirit of the Lord dictate in the choice of the Elders to be Apostles; whereupon all the Elders present expressed their anxious desire to have it so.

"A hymn was then sung, 'Hark, listen to the trumpeters.' President Hyrum Smith prayed, and meeting was dismissed for one hour.

"Assembled pursuant to adjournment, and commenced with prayer.

"President Joseph Smith, Jun., said that the first business of the meeting was, for the Three Witnesses of the Book of Mormon, to pray, each one, and then proceed to choose twelve men from the Church, as Apostles, to go to all nations, kindreds, tongues, and people.

"The Three Witnesses, viz., Oliver Cowdery, David Whitmer, and Martin Harris, united in prayer.

"These Three Witnesses were then blessed by the laying on of the hands of the Presidency.

"The Witnesses then, according to a former commandment, proceeded to make choice of the Twelve. Their names are as follows:

1. Lyman E. Johnson,	7. William E. M'Lellin,
2. Brigham Young,	8. John F. Boynton,
3. Heber C. Kimball,	9. Orson Pratt,
4. Orson Hyde,	10. William Smith,
5. David W. Patten,	11. Thomas B. Marsh,
6. Luke S. Johnson,	12. Parley P. Pratt.

"Lyman E. Johnson, Brigham Young and Heber C. Kimball came forward; and the Three Witnesses laid their hands upon each one's head and prayed, separately." (HC 2:180-87.)

Following the calling and ordination of the Twelve Apostles, Oliver Cowdery was assigned by Joseph Smith to give the newly called Twelve their charge. Parts of this charge are cited here for the sake of illuminating the role of the apostles in this last dispensaton: "Brethren . . . you have been ordained to this holy Priesthood, you have received it from those who have the power and authority from an angel: you are to preach the Gospel to every nation." (HC 2:195.) Oliver Cowdery also challenged each member of the new council to qualify himself as a special witness of the Lord.

In a revelation given to Joseph Smith on March 28, 1835, the Lord explained the following concerning the leadership and government of his church in the last days:

"Of the Melchizedek Priesthood, three Presiding High Priests, chosen by the body, appointed and ordained to that office, and upheld by the confidence, faith, and prayer of the church, form a quorum of the Presidency of the Church.

"The twelve traveling councilors are called to be the Twelve Apostles, or special witnesses of the name of Christ in all the world—thus differing from other officers in the church in the duties of their calling.

"And they form a quorum, equal in authority and power to the three presidents previously mentioned." (D&C 107:22-24.)

The Presidency of the Church was first fully organized as a quorum on March 18, 1833, when Joseph Smith ordained Sidney Rigdon and Frederick G. Williams as his counselors. (See HC 1:334.) This was done in accordance with a revelation given to Joseph Smith on March 8 of that year when the Lord said, "Thus saith the Lord, verily, verily I say unto you my son, thy sins are forgiven thee. . . .

"Therefore, thou art blessed from henceforth that bear the keys of the kingdom given unto you. . . .

"And again, verily I say unto thy brethren, Sidney Rigdon and Frederick G. Williams, their sins are forgiven them also, and they are accounted as equal with thee in holding the keys of this last kingdom." (D&C 90:1-2, 6.)

With regard to the keys and powers to be held jointly by the members of the Presidency and the Twelve by virtue of their ordinations, the Lord said, "And again, the duty of the President of the office of the High Priesthood is to preside over the whole church, and to be like unto Moses—Behold, here is wisdom; yea, to be a seer, a revelator, a translator, and a prophet, having all the gifts of God which he bestows upon the head of the church." (D&C 107:91-92.)

Individually, then, the members of the quorum of the Presidency and the Quorum of the Twelve Apostles receive from the President of the Church the above-mentioned keys, gifts, and powers. They are, as individuals, sustained by the members of the Church as prophets, seers, and revelators according to the direction of the Lord.

As a quorum, the Twelve act under the direction of the Presidency so that order prevails in the kingdom.

Upon the death of the President of the Church, the quorum of the Presidency is dissolved and the Quorum of Twelve becomes the governing council of the Church. They continue to act in this capacity until, under their direction, a new quorum of the First Presidency is organized.

This order of transition in Church leadership was not well understood by the members of the Church at the time of Joseph Smith's martyrdom. As a result there was some momentary confusion over who was to assume the leadership role. This confusion did not exist among the Twelve, however. Brigham Young, who, as president of the Quorum of Twelve Apostles, became the presiding officer of the Church upon the death of the Prophet, understood clearly where the keys of leadership were held. He said, "I have the keys and the means of obtaining the mind of God on the subject.

"I know there are those in our midst who will seek the lives of the Twelve as they did the lives of Joseph and Hyrum. We shall ordain others and give the fulness of the priesthood, so that if we are killed the fulness of the priesthood may remain.

"Joseph conferred upon our heads all the keys and powers belonging to the Apostleship which he himself held before he was taken away, and no man or set of men can get between Joseph and the Twelve in this world or in the world to come." (HC 7:230.)

The Lord provided the members of the Church with a marvelous manifestation to confirm the validity of Brigham Young's position.

"It was while delivering this speech that a transformation of President Brigham Young is said to have occurred, that is to say in voice, person and manner. He seemed to be the personification of Joseph Smith, on the testimony of many who were present. The late President George Q. Cannon of this event said:

" 'If Joseph had arisen from the dead and again spoken in their hearing, the effect could not have been more startling than it was to many present at that meeting; it was the voice of Joseph himself; and not only was it the voice of Joseph which was heard, but it seemed in the eyes of the people as if it were the very person of Joseph which stood before them. A more wonderful and miraculous event than was wrought that day in the presence of that congregation we never heard of. The Lord gave his people a testimony that left no room for doubt as to who was the man chosen to lead them' (*Life of Brigham Young,* Tullidge, 1877, p. 115)." (HC 7:236.)

The same order for transferring leadership in the Church has been followed since the first change in its leadership, when, upon the death of Joseph Smith, Brigham Young and the Twelve asserted the keys given to them. Following the death of Joseph Smith, the Quorum of the First Presidency was not reorganized until December 5, 1847. During the interim the Quorum of the Twelve presided over the Church with Brigham Young as its chief officer. At a conference of the Church in Miller's Hollow near Council Bluffs, Iowa, on the above date, Brigham Young was sustained as President of the Church with Heber C. Kimball as first counselor and Willard Richards as second counselor. This action was later ratified at a general conference of the Church in Salt Lake City on October 8, 1848.

As was the case with the apostles chosen by the Savior in the meridian of time, so it is with the apostles of this final dispensation. They have the power to seal on earth and have it bound in heaven as did Peter and the apostles of old. They hold the keys of authority and power for directing the Lord's work. They are prophets, seers, and revelators. They are the authorized servants of the Lord to conduct the work of building up his church and kingdom in all the earth in preparation for his triumphant return. From them emanate the authority and power to minister in all the affairs of the kingdom. They are the living oracles of God.

47

THE DUTIES
OF THE
MELCHIZEDEK
PRIESTHOOD

Elder Mark E. Petersen

The Holy Priesthood is the power by which mortal men may act in the name of God.

Think of it! The power to act for God! Who can grasp the significance of such a delegation of authority? Who can measure such a privilege?

The entire plan of salvation is embraced in priesthood functions. Without the priesthood there would be no salvation, for it is through the Church that the Lord saves his faithful people, and it is through the priesthood—men called of God as was Aaron—that the Church fulfills its divine destiny.

The apostle Paul made this clear in his epistle to the Ephesians as he described the organization of the Church, saying that it is literally "built upon the foundation of the apostles and prophets, Jesus Christ himself being the chief corner stone." He went on to say that the Church thus constituted was "fitly framed together," growing into an "holy temple in the Lord." (Ephesians 2:20-21.)

This is significant. It shows how truly important to the Church are the labors of the men and boys who hold the priesthood.

Four major areas of responsibility were laid upon priesthood brethren in ancient times. They are equally binding upon us who live today. Those primary responsibilities are:

1. To so live the gospel personally that each holder of the priesthood will be fully worthy to officiate in his callings.

2. To actively labor in the Church and build up the kingdom of God here on earth.

3. To preach the gospel to every nation, kindred, tongue, and people.

4. To perform vicarious work for the salvation of the dead.

When Paul listed the names of some of the officers in the Church, he made it clear that apostles, prophets, evangelists, pastors, and teachers were placed in the Church purposely to *act for God* as his agents in bringing about the salvation of his people. He mentioned their obligations as follows:

1. Perfecting the saints by edifying and instructing them.

2. Conducting the work of the ministry.

3. Developing a unity of the faith and an increased knowledge of the Son of God among the members of the Church.

4. Protecting the saints from false teachers, "that we henceforth be no more children tossed to and fro, and carried about by every wind of doctrine."

5. Preserving the truth through the medium of love, thus growing up unto Christ in all things. (Ephesians 4:12-15.)

The Savior, however, opened an even wider vista by introducing his worldwide missionary program, which became a major duty of the priesthood. Said the Lord: "Go ye therefore, and teach all nations, baptizing them in the name of the Father, and of the Son, and of the Holy Ghost: Teaching them to observe all things whatsoever I have commanded you." (Matthew 28:19-20.)

But there is still that other dimension—temple work for the dead.

Paul knew about baptism for the dead (1 Corinthians 15:29), and Peter revealed that Christ went to the world of departed spirits while his body lay in the tomb, and preached the gospel there. He gave the reason for it also: "For for this cause was the gospel preached also to them that are dead, that they might be judged according to men in the flesh, but live according to God in the spirit." (1 Peter 4:6.)

What, then, are the duties related to the Holy Priesthood? They may be summarized as follows: (1) strengthening the established church; (2) preaching the gospel to the world; and (3) laboring for our dead.

All three responsibilities require the exercise of priesthood, primarily that of the Melchizedek order.

The Perfecting of the Saints

Perfection begins with ourselves. We ourselves must obey the gospel rules. But we are also called upon to assist others to reach that goal. Living the gospel is required of each member. Priesthood officers are to assist others to understand and live its truths so that they in turn may labor toward perfection.

The teacher must first obey, or how can the pupil believe? We cannot require others to do what we ourselves fail to do. Hence our first duty is to obey the gospel in our own lives.

In the oath and covenant of the priesthood we agree to "live by every word that proceedeth forth from the mouth of God." (D&C 84:44.)

Solomon put it this way: "Let us hear the conclusion of the whole matter: Fear God, and keep his commandments: for this is the whole duty of man." (Ecclesiastes 12:13.)

Paul knew that to function in the priesthood, a man must live the gospel. It is that which qualifies him for his priestly labors. So Paul listed these important duties:

1. "Walk not as other Gentiles walk, in the vanity of their mind."
2. Put off your former manner of life, with its deceitful lusts.
3. "Put on the new man, which after God is created in righteousness and true holiness."
4. Put away lying, and "speak every man the truth."
5. "Let not the sun go down upon your wrath."
6. "Let him that stole steal no more."
7. Labor in honor, working that which is good and giving to him who has need.
8. Let no corrupt speech proceed out of your mouth, but speak to others that which is edifying.
9. "Let all bitterness, and wrath, and anger, and clamour, and evil speaking, be put away from you."
10. "Be ye kind one to another, tenderhearted, forgiving."
11. "Grieve not the Holy Spirit." (See Ephesians 4:17-32.)

Then what is the first and most basic duty of the holder of the priesthood? It is to be *worthy* to hold and use it!

President Joseph F. Smith said concerning worthiness in the priesthood: "The Priesthood of the Son of God cannot be exercised in any degree of unrighteousness; neither will its power, its virtue and authority abide with him who is corrupt, who is treacherous in his soul toward God and toward his fellowmen. It will not abide in force and power with him who does not honor it in his life by complying with the requirements of heaven." (*Gospel Doctrine*, Deseret Book, 1939, p. 160.)

Out of the Best Books

Intellectual preparation to function in the priesthood is also necessary. It is our duty to study and know the reason for our faith. The Lord commands it. He so instructed Hyrum Smith, brother of the Prophet Joseph:

"Wait a little longer, until you shall have my word . . . that you may know of a surety my doctrine. . . . Seek not to declare my word, but first seek to obtain my word, and then shall your tongue be loosed." (D&C 11:16, 21.)

And what did the Savior say to his ancient disciples? "Learn of me." (Matthew 11:29.) "Search the scriptures." (John 5:39.) "This is life eternal, that they might know thee the only true God, and Jesus Christ, whom thou hast sent." (John 17:3.)

A solemn duty of holders of the priesthood is to become well informed in the gospel so that they may use their priesthood intelligently for the perfection and instruction of their fellow Church members and others seeking to know the truth.

In Kirtland the Lord said to the Saints: "And as all have not faith, seek ye diligently and teach one another words of wisdom; yea, seek ye out of the best books words of wisdom, seek learning even by study and also by faith." (D&C 109:7.) It is a duty imposed upon us by the Lord.

At another time he gave this instruction:

"And I give unto you a commandment that you shall teach one another the doctrine of the kingdom.

51

"Teach ye diligently and my grace shall attend you, that you may be instructed more perfectly in theory, in principle, in doctrine, in the law of the gospel, in all things that pertain unto the kingdom of God, that are expedient for you to understand;

"Of things both in heaven and in earth, and under the earth; things which have been, things which are, things which must shortly come to pass; things which are at home, things which are abroad; the wars and the perplexities of the nations, and the judgments which are on the land; and a knowledge also of countries and of kingdoms—

"That ye may be prepared in all things when I shall send you again to magnify the calling whereunto I have called you, and the mission with which I have commissioned you." (D&C 88:77-80.)

Knowing how to perform the ordinances is necessary also. All holders of the Melchizedek Priesthood should learn how to consecrate oil, how to anoint the sick, and how to confirm an anointing as they administer to the sick. They should know how to baptize, how to confirm new members in the Church, and how to bless the sacrament.

Holders of the priesthood should understand quorum procedures and the functions of the various organizations. If they are so prepared, they may officiate intelligently wherever they are called.

In the early days of the Church the Prophet Joseph established schools and a university in Nauvoo. He believed in preparation through education. One of his most important achievements in this regard was the establishment of the school of the prophets, wherein the brethren not only studied scripture and the doctrines given by the prophet, but also various languages and the geography and government of other countries.

A well-informed priesthood is necessary to a successful administration.

Perfection in the Home
Our effort to seek perfection must, of course, reach into and become a part of our homes.

Within the family, the priesthood holder should show what a Christlike life really is. Love at home is basic. First and foremost is the affection that must prevail between husband and wife.

The Lord laid down a strict law in this regard when he said: "Thou shalt love thy wife with all thy heart, and shalt cleave unto her and none else." (D&C 42:22.) President Spencer W Kimball has explained that the converse is also true: The wife should love her husband with all her heart and cleave to him and none else.

Such affection would provide an atmosphere of love and devotion in which children may be reared successfully. They would learn by example and come to understand the value of true affection in the home. Proper relationships would then exist between parents and children, and among the children themselves.

If all husbands and wives lived this way, there would be very few, if any, family quarrels, or instances of abuse of husband or wife, or cruelty to children, or of divorce.

The priesthood-holding husband would take the lead in setting the spiritual atmosphere of the home. It is his duty to do so. There would be daily prayers; there would be systematic study of the scriptures, and regular observance of the Sabbath and of the home evening. All these are included among our priesthood duties.

The teachings in the home would stress virtue, honesty, kindness, and obedience. Respect for the law would be upheld. Honoring Church leaders would become a family trait. We would be willing to take active part in ward affairs. If we are to teach others, we must live these principles ourselves.

The Lord gives us his definition of the Christlike life in section 4 of the Doctrine and Covenants. He lists the following attributes:

Faith, hope, charity and love,
An eye single to the glory of God,
Virtue, knowledge, temperance, patience,
    brotherly kindness,
Godliness, humility, diligence.

Applying these principles to the conduct of his own family, the priesthood holder would cherish and cooperate with his wife; he would teach his children properly; he would provide meaningful companionship for them all; and in every way he would set the example of a Christlike life.

The Lord gives these specific references pertaining to the rearing of children:

"Every member of the church of Christ having children is to bring them unto the elders before the church, who are to lay their hands upon them in the name of Jesus Christ, and bless them in his name." (D&C 20:70.)

"And again, inasmuch as parents have children in Zion, or in any of her stakes which are organized, that teach them not to understand the doctrine of repentance, faith in Christ the Son of the living God, and of baptism and the gift of the Holy Ghost by the laying on of the hands, when eight years old, the sin be upon the heads of the parents.

"For this shall be a law unto the inhabitants of Zion, or in any of her stakes which are organized.

"And their children shall be baptized for the remission of their sins when eight years old, and receive the laying on of the hands.

"And they shall also teach their children to pray, and to walk uprightly before the Lord.

"And the inhabitants of Zion shall also observe the Sabbath day to keep it holy." (D&C 68:25-29.)

The Work of the Ministry

Each quorum is presided over by its own officers, as is true also of the auxiliary work for men and boys. Quorums function in close harmony with bishops in carrying out the priesthood duties of the ward, just as they cooperate with stake presidents in assignments coming from them.

The Lord was very specific in outlining the duties of priesthood holders in the restored Church. They are set forth primarily in sections 20 and 107 of the Doctrine and Covenants, although other sections provide additional instruction.

Duties of elders, priests, teachers, and deacons are partially interrelated. Among these responsibilities are preaching the gospel, converting and baptizing believers, bestowing the gift of the Holy Ghost, administering the sacrament of the Lord's Supper, watching over the Church always, visiting the house of each member and exhorting them to pray and attend to all family duties.

The priesthood brethren are to see that the Saints meet together often and do their duty in the Church. They are to see that there is no iniquity in the Church, "neither hardness with each other, neither lying, backbiting, nor evil speaking." (D&C 20:54-55.)

Conferences of the Church are to be conducted by the presiding priesthood brethren. Once a year conferences are held in each ward, twice a year in each stake, and twice a year in Salt Lake City for the entire Church.

One of the important matters of business in these conferences is the approval of those brethren who will be given the priesthood or advanced by ordination. As in other matters, the law of common consent is invoked in this procedure, and all whose names are presented are voted on by the congregation.

The Lord specifically says that "no person is to be ordained to any office in this church, where there is a regularly organized branch of the same, without the vote of that church." (D&C 20:65.)

He expanded on that instruction when he said: "And all things shall be done by common consent in the church, by much prayer and faith, for all things you shall receive by faith." (D&C 26:2.)

He made it even more clear when he gave this:

"The above offices I have given unto you, and the keys thereof, for helps and for governments, for the work of the ministry and the perfecting of my saints.

"And a commandment I give unto you, that you should fill all these offices and approve of those names which I have mentioned, or else disapprove of them at my general conference." (D&C 124:143-44.)

As a further direction to the priesthood, the Lord by revelation said that there should be no idlers among the Saints, and that they should labor earnestly, without greed, not for the things of this world, but for the riches of eternity. (D&C 68:29-31.)

Teaching these principles and carrying them out in their own lives is one of the duties of the priesthood.

Presiding officers are common judges in Israel, particularly the bishops and stake presidents. The Lord gave instruction that "any member of the church of Christ transgressing, or being overtaken in a fault, shall be dealt with as the scriptures direct." (D&C 20:80.)

The duties of seventies and high priests are clearly set forth in section 107 of the Doctrine and Covenants. The high priests, like the elders, are to be standing ministers in the Church. The seventy become traveling ministers to preach the gospel and conduct the affairs of the Church in all the world.

In defining the work of the seventies, the Lord said further:

"Which quorum is instituted for traveling elders to bear record of my name in all the world, wherever the traveling high council, mine apostles, shall send them to prepare a way before my face.

"The difference between this quorum and the quorum of the elders is that one is to travel continually, and the other is to preside over the churches from time to time; the one has the responsibility of presiding from time to time, and the other has no responsibility of presiding, saith the Lord your God." (D&C 124:139-40.)

The ministry of the priesthood includes, of course, the labors of the Twelve Apostles of the Lamb. They are the traveling "high council" to administer and set in order the affairs of the Church "in all the world."

The First Presidency, who are the presiding high priests over all the Church, are indeed prophets, seers, and revelators. They receive the needed guidance from heaven pertaining to all activities and responsibilities in the Church. They are the leaders of us all. They direct in all things. In this general supervision of the entire kingdom of God on earth, they are assisted by the Council of the Twelve.

When the First Presidency is disorganized by the death of

the president, the Twelve temporarily become the governing body of the Church. Theirs is the responsibility of "directing all things" in this interim. But the Lord provided that there shall be but a short time between the death of the president of the Church and the selection of his successor.

The custom, therefore, is that the Council of the Twelve meets soon after the final rites for the deceased leader and proceeds to set apart the new president, who always is the president of the Twelve now advanced to the new position.

Since the Twelve preside over the Church during the interim period, and the president of the Twelve presides over the Twelve, it becomes a simple procedure to install the president of the Twelve as the president of the Church when the First Presidency is reconstituted. His advancement from the Twelve to the First Presidency comes by action of the Twelve, after which, at the next general conference of the Church, the new First Presidency is sustained by the membership at large.

The next senior apostle then becomes the president of the Twelve, and the work proceeds in the normal way once again.

The reconstitution of the First Presidency is probably the most important duty of the Council of the Twelve.

As the Lord sums up his instructions to his priesthood he says:

"Wherefore, now let every man learn his duty, and to act in the office in which he is appointed, in all diligence.

"He that is slothful shall not be counted worthy to stand, and he that learns not his duty and shows himself not approved shall not be counted worthy to stand." (D&C 107:99-100.)

The Missionary Program

One of the earliest assignments the Lord gave to the Church as it was restored was that the brethren should begin an immediate and extensive missionary program.

The gospel must go to all the world, and the Prophet Joseph Smith set out to do that very thing. He began preaching the gospel even before the Church was organized on

April 6, 1830, and as a result, many believed and were present when the six selected brethren formed the Church by formal and legal action.

Immediately afterward the Prophet began sending missionaries abroad. He himself became the first and most constant missionary of them all.

Elders were sent to the neighboring counties and states. Others were sent abroad. Most of the apostles went for a time to Great Britain, where a rich harvest was found. Elders were sent also to South America and the South Sea islands. And Orson Hyde was sent to Palestine to dedicate that land for the return of the Jews.

Joseph himself preached extensively in the United States and Canada. Often he was gone for weeks at a time in his missionary endeavor, while keeping in touch with Church headquarters and his own family as best he could.

When the Saints moved west, the pattern was continued. Married men made up most of the missionary force in those days. Families cooperated to help each other. Wives cheerfully sent their husbands abroad and took up the family labors themselves. Who else could be sent on missions? The youth of the Church were not yet ready, so the fathers had to assume the burden.

Between December 2, 1920, and December 24, 1921, President David O. McKay, then of the Council of the Twelve, accompanied by Hugh J. Cannon, president of Liberty Stake, visited most countries and missions on a world tour. Nation after nation was dedicated by President McKay for the preaching of the gospel. This included both China and Japan.

In November of 1925, Elders Melvin J. Ballard of the Council of the Twelve and Rey L. Pratt and Rulon S. Wells of the First Council of the Seventy, were sent to South America to open the work there. In a park in the heart of Buenos Aires, Elder Ballard dedicated all of South America for the preaching of the gospel. Since then the work has been taken to all parts of that land, and today we have stakes and missions dotting the entire continent.

The work in Mexico and Central America has been

highly responsive, as it has been also in Hawaii, Australia, New Zealand, and the islands of the South Pacific.

Today with more than 30,000 missionaries in more than seventy nations, the work is proceeding rapidly, with hundreds of thousands of converts being brought into the fold.

Most of the present-day missionaries are young men between nineteen and twenty-one years of age. Many young women twenty-one years and older accept mission calls. Hundreds of married couples who have raised their families and find it possible to leave their homes are sent on missions from one end of the world to the other, from Alaska to South Africa, from Australia to Finland.

The Church takes seriously the Lord's command to go into every nation and preach the gospel.

Not only did the Savior in ancient times command that the gospel should be carried abroad to all peoples, but he also repeated this instruction to his modern disciples:

"And now, verily saith the Lord, that these things might be known among you, O inhabitants of the earth, I have sent forth mine angel flying through the midst of heaven, having the everlasting gospel, who hath appeared unto some and hath committed it unto man, who shall appear unto many that dwell on the earth.

"And this gospel shall be preached unto every nation, and kindred, and tongue, and people.

"And the servants of God shall go forth, saying with a loud voice: Fear God and give glory to him, for the hour of his judgment is come;

"And worship him that made heaven, and earth, and the sea, and the fountains of waters." (D&C 133:36-39.)

When the Prophet Joseph was still at Hiram, Ohio, the Lord gave similar direction:

"Go ye into all the world, preach the gospel to every creature, acting in the authority which I have given you, baptizing in the name of the Father, and of the Son, and of the Holy Ghost.

"And he that believeth and is baptized shall be saved, and he that believeth not shall be damned.

"And he that believeth shall be blest with signs following, even as it is written.

"And unto you it shall be given to know the signs of the times, and the signs of the coming of the Son of Man;

"And of as many as the Father shall bear record, to you shall be given power to seal them up unto eternal life." (D&C 68:8-12.)

The First Presidency of today, like their predecessors, obey this injunction. Hence the constant call for more missionaries; hence the need to translate our printed works into more and more languages; hence the use of even satellite radio and television transmission to reach the far corners of the earth.

The Lord commands—his servants obey—and the word goes abroad to all who will hear.

Salvation for the Dead
Salvation for the dead falls into two categories: genealogical research wherein we identify the dead, and ordinance work in the temples whereby the saving rites of the gospel are performed for them by proxy.

Whereas all members—and even nonmembers—may be engaged in genealogical research, the temple service is strictly ordinance work, and this requires the proper function of the holy priesthood.

The Church is far and beyond the greatest and most active genealogical organization in the world. Starting out in a small way at first, it is now international in its scope. Nations cooperate in the microfilming of vital records in most parts of the world. These records are stored in vaults in Salt Lake City for safekeeping, but copies are distributed to several hundred branch libraries. There they are used both for the extraction programs whereby all names are taken off and for private research by individuals and families.

High priests quorums have been given the responsibility to stimulate interest in genealogical research, and as a result, millions of family names are being provided.

Temple work is for both the living and the dead. All ordinances of the temple are essential saving ordinances, even as is baptism. They are required for our ultimate exaltation in the kingdom of God.

Temples now are being made available to people in many lands. More are being constructed both in the United States and on other hemispheres. As this construction work proceeds, Saints in all parts of the world may receive their endowments and sealings. Then as they complete these ordinances for themselves, they may do a similar but vicarious work for the dead.

This is one of the greatest duties of the Saints. It is one of the primary duties of the priesthood of the Church, for without the priesthood none of it would be possible. Individual holders of the priesthood and quorums alike are expected to assume this great responsibility, knowing that we without our dead cannot be made perfect, and neither can our dead receive perfection without us.

THE
BISHOP

Bishop Victor L. Brown

Before I became a bishop, I knew little about the responsibilities of the office. The bishop is, or should be, one of the most important persons in the life of every member of the Church. If he is important to us, then we must be important to him.

To understand the bishop, we must know something of his responsibilities. They are many, so we will discuss only a few. First, we will review two of his temporal responsibilities —*care of the needy* and *finances.*

Frequently we hear the statement, in connection with the welfare program, that the Church takes care of its own. The bishop plays the key role in administering the welfare program. He, and he alone, determines who will receive assistance, in what form it will be, and, with the help of the Relief Society president, how much.

The bishop approaches this assignment in a spirit of love, kindness, and understanding. One of his prime goals is to help the persons who need assistance to maintain their self-respect and dignity. He has certain principles upon which he administers the program.

The first principle is that we as members of the Church are expected to be self-reliant and independent. We are taught to have a year's supply in reserve in case of serious difficulty. Should circumstances, such as a serious accident or illness, result in our needing help, we should look to our families. If they cannot or will not help, only then should we look to the bishop.

After a very careful, personal investigation, the bishop decides whether the Church should render assistance. If he decides it should, the assistance will be limited to the necessities of life, and only for immediate needs. The bishop is not expected to bail us out of financial difficulty caused by poor management of our affairs.

If he gives assistance, he will expect us to work for it if we are physically able. His motive here is to help us maintain our self-respect by not accepting a dole. Frankly, many times it would be much easier for him to give a dole. But he recognizes the dole as an evil, and it is his desire to bless us with the program, not weaken us.

There are many other facets of the program, such as fast offering, welfare production projects, and bishops' storehouses. As members of the Church, we are expected to respond to the call of the bishop and his welfare committee in each phase of the program. In some areas of the world the welfare program is conducted on a limited basis. In these cases, we are still expected to support the bishop within the established policies.

Now as to finances: The bishop must look to the members of his ward for the financial support necessary to carry on the affairs of the ward.

One of the worrisome problems some bishops have is collecting funds for the ward budget. These are the funds that are needed to operate the ward organizations and to share in the costs of maintaining the chapel. We, as members of the ward, can offer great assistance to the bishop if we will be responsive to his requests for financial assistance. The Lord said he would open the windows of heaven and pour out blessings that there would hardly be room enough to receive, if we would pay our tithes and offerings.

The bishop realizes that all funds collected by him are sacred, and that they come as free-will offerings. Through our willingness to sustain him in financial matters, we help lighten his load.

So far we have discussed only temporal matters. Now let us review some of his spiritual responsibilities.

The bishop, by revelation from the Lord, is the president of the priests quorum. He and his counselors constitute the presidency of the Aaronic Priesthood in his ward. He is the cornerstone in all matters pertaining to the youth, both boys and girls. He receives help from his counselors, home teachers, advisers, auxiliary officers and teachers; but he is still the keystone in all that is done.

To the young people may I say that the bishop has been called through the inspiration of our Heavenly Father to be your spiritual counselor. He is designated by the Lord as a common judge. He has a special blessing, giving him the power of discernment and understanding. He is the one to whom we should go to confess our sins. This must be done if we are to repent fully.

The bishop recognizes that it is through the blessings of the Lord that he is a judge, and unless he is a righteous judge, he is liable to condemnation, for in the scriptures we read "that the rights of the priesthood are inseparably connected with the powers of heaven, and that the powers of heaven cannot be controlled nor handled only upon the principles of righteousness.

"That they may be conferred upon us, it is true; but when we undertake to cover our sins, or to gratify our pride, our vain ambition, or to exercise control or dominion or compulsion upon the souls of the children of men, in any degree of unrighteousness, behold, the heavens withdraw themselves; the Spirit of the Lord is grieved; and when it is withdrawn, Amen to the priesthood or the authority of that man." (D&C 121:36-37.)

The bishop is unalterably opposed to sin in any guise; at the same time, he has great understanding and compassion for the sinner. He recognizes many problems of life and is anxious to lend a helping hand, particularly when the going is difficult. He can help you in many ways if you will just let him. Anything you disclose to your bishop is expected to be kept as a sacred trust. May I encourage you to let your bishop bless you with his wisdom. Get close to him. He will never be too busy to help you.

There is another basic spiritual responsibility that encompasses all others: The bishop is the spiritual father of the ward, the presiding high priest. This responsibility spreads his umbrella wide enough to cover us all.

He has a host of helpers to assist him in this. They are the home teachers. This is a responsibility of the priesthood holder that, if carried out devotedly, will lift a great load from the bishop's shoulders. The home teacher is in reality an assistant to the bishop. He is the major contact with the family. One bishop made the comment that one of the highest compliments he had been paid was to have a family call their home teacher first in the case of sickness. President David O. McKay stated that if the home teachers were doing their duty, in the case of a death in the family they would be called first, not the bishop. May I encourage each home teacher to sense his responsibility and carry out his duty as an assistant to the bishop.

As the father of the ward, the bishop has many other helpers. Each officer and teacher in the ward assists him. We, as ward members, have a responsibility to respond to calls from our bishop. He should be able to depend on us to carry out our assignments. He needs the help of all of us. With that help, not only does the work of the Lord progress, but we individually are blessed, for "When ye are in the service of your fellow beings ye are only in the service of your God." (Mosiah 2:17.)

Who is this bishop we have been talking about? He may be the neighbor next door; he may be the son of your close friends; he may be that noisy boy you had in your Sunday School class just a few years ago—you remember, the one you were ready to send out, never to come back.

He almost always is a husband, generally a father, always a breadwinner. He is faced with all of the problems you and I have. He has his human frailties and weaknesses, his likes and dislikes, maybe even some idiosyncrasies. Yes, he is a human being—a special human being because of a special calling with a special blessing. Here is what the Lord said he must be: "A bishop then must be blameless, the husband of one wife, vigilant, sober, of good behaviour, given to hospitality, apt to teach;

"Not given to wine, no striker, not greedy of filthy lucre; but patient, not a brawler, not covetous;

"One that ruleth well his own house, having his children in subjection with all gravity;

"(For if a man know not how to rule his own house, how shall he take care of the church of God?)

"Not a novice, lest being lifted up with pride he fall into the condemnation of the devil." (1 Timothy 3:2-6.)

This man, your bishop, did not ask for this position; he did not even volunteer. He most likely accepted the calling with fear and trembling, yet with the faith and desire to per- fect himself so as to measure up to that which the Lord ex- pects of him.

His loyal, loving wife and his children have also agreed to share in his responsibility with him, by not complaining when he is away from home so much of the time, by being cheerful when the telephone rings at dinner time or three o'clock in the morning, and by being willing to carry some of the responsibility that normally belongs to the husband and father.

May the Lord's choicest blessings be showered upon the heads of these wonderful, devoted bishops, their wives, and their children; and may we, the members of their wards, respond to their leadership. The Lord will bless us for sus- taining the servants he has called to preside over us.

PRIESTHOOD COURTS: COURTS OF LOVE

Elder Robert L. Simpson

The hour was very late; the room was quiet except for the audible sobs of a young man who had just received the verdict of a Church court. Justice had taken its true course. There was apparently no alternative. The unanimous decision, following serious deliberation, fasting, and prayer, was excommunication.

After several minutes, a weary face looked up, and the young man's voice broke the silence as he said, "I have just lost the most precious thing in my life, and nothing will stand in my way until I have regained it."

The process leading up to the court was not an easy one. Certainly, courage is a most important factor for every person who has seriously slipped but wants to get back on the Lord's side.

After the meeting was finished, the communications that followed the young man's dramatic statement of hope for the future were so reassuring. From some there were firm promises of help during the ensuing months of continuing repentance; from others a pat on the back and a handshake, with an eye-to-eye assurance that conveyed a feeling of confidence and the hand of fellowship. There was complete knowledge among all present at that meeting that all could be regained in the life of this young man if it were done in the Lord's way.

This young man had just taken his first giant step back. As an excommunicated member of the Church and with his heart determined to make things right, he was far better off than just a few days before with his membership record intact but carrying deceit in his heart that seemed to shout the word *hypocrite* with every move he made toward doing something in the Church.

This episode took place a few years ago. The young man's

pledge has been fulfilled, and in my opinion, no member of the Church stands on ground more firm than the man who has had the courage to unburden himself to his priesthood authority and to set things in order with his Master. What a relief to have once again the peace of mind that "passeth all understanding."

Priesthood courts of the Church are not courts of retribution. They are courts of love. Oh, that members of the Church could understand this fact!

The adversary places a fear in the heart of the transgressor that makes it so difficult for him to do what needs to be done; and in the words of Elder James E. Talmage, "As the time of repentance is procrastinated, the ability to repent grows weaker; neglect of opportunity in holy things develops inability." (*Articles of Faith*, p. 114.) This simply means that doing what needs to be done will never be easier than right now. As in all other paths and guideposts that have been provided for us to achieve our eternal destiny of exaltation, there are no shortcuts.

Heavenly Father is not antiprogress: he is the author of eternal progression. In his own words, "Behold, this is my work and my glory—to bring to pass the immortality and eternal life of man." (Moses 1:39.)

Our achievement of eternal life adds glory to his name and is the only ultimate objective acceptable to a true Latter-day Saint.

Reduced to its simplest terms, our mission here in mortality is to overcome weaknesses of the flesh and all irregularities in our lives to the point that our control of personal desires is sufficient to bring about a daily living and thinking pattern that will be compatible with his holy presence.

Be not disillusioned by doctrine of the adversary that there will likely be a magic point in eternity when all of a sudden selfish and improper actions are automatically eliminated from our being. Holy writ has confirmed time and time again that such is not the case, and prophets through the ages have assured us that now is the time to repent, right here in this mortal sphere. It will never be easier than now; and returning to Brother Talmage's thought, he who procrastinates that day or hopes for an alternate method that might require less courage waits in vain, and in the meantime, the possibilities grow dimmer. He is playing the game as Satan would have him play it, and exaltation in the presence of God grows more remote with each passing day.

To each of our bishops we say: Be available to your people. Let them know about the kindness and compassion that dominates your soul. Don't become so caught up in the business affairs of your ward administration that you fail to convey to your people all of those wonderful attributes referred to in section 121 of the Doctrine and Covenants. I am talking about the attributes of kindly persuasion, long-suffering, gentleness, meekness, and love unfeigned.

Bishop, learn the great principle of delegation so that your heart and your mind can be free to counsel with the Saints. You are their common judge. There is no one else in the entire ward so designated by the Lord. It is you to whom they must turn. You must be available to listen, and, equally important, you must live in such a way that the voice of heaven will find utterance through you for the blessing and edification of your people.

I am certain that a basic cornerstone of true justice is compassion. Perhaps even more important than the transgression itself is the sensitivity of a person's soul and his desire to repent and to follow the Master.

It would be so much easier to talk about serious transgression to someone you had never seen before and would likely never see again; or, better still, to talk in total seclusion to an unseen ear and receive your forgiveness then and there from unseen lips. But in such a process, who would then be at your side in the struggling months ahead, as you attempt with great effort to make your repentance complete, as you strive to prevent a tragic recurrence?

Few, if any, men have the strength to climb that hill alone, and please be assured, it is uphill all the way. There needs to be help—someone who really loves you, someone who has been divinely commissioned to assist you confidentially, quietly, assuredly—and may I reemphasize the word *confidentially*, for here again, Satan has spread the false rumor that confidences are rarely kept.

May I assure you that bishops and stake presidents are not in the habit of betraying these sacred confidences. Before being ordained and set apart, their very lives have been reviewed in that upper room in the temple by those divinely called as prophets, seers, and revelators. Without question, they are among the noble and great ones of this world, and they should be regarded as such by the Saints.

What a glorious plan this is! How reassuring to know that we all have hope for a total blessing, in spite of all the mistakes we have made; that there might be complete fulfillment; that we might enter His holy presence with our family units.

Even excommunication from this church is not the end of the world; and if this process is necessary in carrying out true justice, I bear you my personal and solemn witness that even this extreme penalty of excommunication can be the first giant step back, provided there follows a sincere submission to the Spirit and faith in the authenticity of God's plan.

These processes can be carried out in this church only through properly designated priesthood authority, for His house is a house of order. All of this is made very clear in the Doctrine and Covenants. May I quote:

"And again, verily I say unto you, that which is governed by law is also preserved by law and perfected and sanctified by the same.

"That which breaketh a law, and abideth not by law, but seeketh to become a law unto itself, and willeth to abide in sin, and altogether abideth in sin, cannot be sanctified by law, neither by mercy, justice, nor judgment. Therefore, they must remain filthy still.

"All kingdoms have a law given;

"And there are many kingdoms; for there is no space in the which there is no kingdom; and there is no kingdom in which there is no space, either a greater or a lesser kingdom.

"And unto every kingdom is given a law; and unto every law there are certain bounds also and conditions.

"All beings who abide not in those conditions are not justified." (D&C 88:34-39.)

In other words, all beings who abide not in those conditions, all who fail to correct infractions of the eternal law by proper priesthood procedures that have been established for such corrections, are unacceptable to the Lord and will likely never be eligible for his presence.

God bless us to accept eternal law and understand that there can be no other way.

THE AARONIC PRIESTHOOD

Elder M. Russell Ballard

When Wilford Woodruff served on a mission in Arkansas and Tennessee in 1834, his life was spared and he was taught in a most dramatic way by an angel of the Lord. At that time he held the office of priest in the Aaronic Priesthood. Regarding his experience he said:

"I travelled thousands of miles and preached the Gospel as a priest, and, as I have said to congregations before, the Lord sustained me and made manifest His power in the defense of my life as much while I held that office as He has done while I hold the office of an apostle. The Lord sustains any man that holds a portion of the Priesthood, whether he is a Priest, an Elder, a Seventy, or an Apostle, if he magnifies his calling and does his duty." (*Millennial Star*, September 28, 1905, p. 610.)

The Aaronic Priesthood held by young men from twelve years of age to eighteen is still in force today with all the majesty and power in its offices and callings. It is called the lesser priesthood "because it is an appendage to the greater, or the Melchizedek Priesthood." (D&C 107:14.) Since all priesthood is Melchizedek, the Aaronic Priesthood being a portion of it, one does not lose the Aaronic Priesthood when he is ordained to the Melchizedek Priesthood, and the same diligence is required in its offices and callings as in the greater priesthood.

The Aaronic Priesthood Anciently

When Moses spoke with the Lord face to face on Mount Sinai after the Exodus from Egypt, he was directed to call Aaron, who held the Melchizedek Priesthood, to a new assignment in the priesthood: "And thou shalt command the children of Israel, that they bring thee pure oil olive beaten for the light, to cause the lamp to burn always. In the tabernacle of the congregation without the vail, which is before the testimony, Aaron and his sons shall order it from evening to morning before the Lord: it shall be a statute for ever unto their generations on the behalf of the children of Israel." (Exodus 27:20-21.)

The Lord further directed that Aaron and his four sons would become priests in an appendant order of the priesthood: "And take thou unto thee Aaron thy brother, and his sons with him, from among the children of Israel, that he may minister unto me in the priest's office." (Exodus 28:1.)

This new order of the priesthood is what we know today as the Aaronic Priesthood.

The Priesthood of Aaron "has power in administering outward ordinances" of the gospel. (D&C 107:14.) When a young man is ordained to that priesthood, he has power to administer in those ordinances of salvation which are assigned to that priesthood. Literally, a young man so called and ordained has the power and authority to act in the name of the Lord in performing the ordinances of the Aaronic Priesthood.

The ancient holders of the Aaronic Priesthood administered numerous ordinances that were set forth as part of the law given unto ancient Israel. These ordinances were given to ancient Israel to help prepare them to accept Christ when he came.

The Prophet Joseph Smith, in a discourse in the Nauvoo Temple on January 29, 1843, answered a question regarding John's position of greatness:

"How is it that John was considered one of the greatest of prophets? His miracles could not have constituted his greatness.

"First. He was entrusted with a divine mission of preparing the way before the face of the Lord. Whoever had such a trust committed to him before or since? No man.

"Secondly. He was entrusted with the important mission, and it was required at his hands, to baptize the Son of Man. Whoever had the honor of doing that? Whoever had so great a privilege and glory? Whoever led the Son of God into the waters of baptism, and had the privilege of behold-

73

ing the Holy Ghost descend in the form of a dove, or rather in the *sign* of the dove, in witness of that administration? . . .

Aaron and his sons acted in the full power and authority of the Aaronic Priesthood. Many of their functions would be comparable to our present-day bishops and priests in the Church. Those righteous Levites who were given the priesthood probably functioned in somewhat the same manner as teachers and deacons in that they collected the tithes of the people (Hebrews 7:5) and participated in sacrifices (although today the sacrament is administered instead of blood sacrifice).

After Moses was taken unto the Lord, the Melchizedek Priesthood was also taken from the midst of the people, but "all the prophets had the Melchizedek Priesthood and were ordained by God himself." (*Teachings of the Prophet Joseph Smith*, p. 181.) Moses was the presiding authority over the Melchizedek Priesthood until he was taken from the earth.

"Therefore, he [the Lord] took Moses out of their midst, and the Holy Priesthood also; and the lesser priesthood continued, which priesthood holdeth the key of the ministering of angels and the preparatory gospel; which gospel is the gospel of repentance and of baptism, and the remission of sins, and the law of carnal commandments, which the Lord in his wrath caused to continue with the house of Aaron among the children of Israel until John, whom God raised up, being filled with the Holy Ghost from his mother's womb." (D&C 84:25-27.)

The John who is referred to is John the Baptist, who was the last person on earth to hold the keys of the Aaronic Priesthood until the time he restored them to Joseph Smith and Oliver Cowdery. John held these keys because of the hereditary nature of the Aaronic Priesthood and its keys from Aaron until the time of John. "And the Lord confirmed a priesthood also upon Aaron and his seed, throughout all their generations." (D&C 84:18.)

John the Baptist was a direct descendant of Aaron and held the keys of the Aaronic Priesthood. (*Teachings of the Prophet Joseph Smith*, pp. 272-73.) He received a special ordination to the work he was to perform: "For he was baptized while he was yet in his childhood, and was ordained by the angel of God at the time he was eight days old unto this power . . . to prepare them [his people] for the coming of the Lord, in whose hand is given all power." (D&C 84:28.)

As the last legal administrator of the Aaronic Priesthood in the Mosaic dispensation, John was called to prepare the way of the Lord. "He had the keys of the Aaronic Priesthood, and although he was a priest, his position, like that of Aaron before him, was comparable to the office of the presiding bishop in his Aaronic Priesthood responsibilities." (Oscar W. McConkie, *The Aaronic Priesthood*, Deseret Book, 1977, p. 31.)

The greatest praise of John's earthly mission came from Jesus, who stated that "there is not a greater prophet than John the Baptist." (Luke 7:28.)

"Thirdly. John, at that time, was the only legal administrator in the affairs of the kingdom there was then on the earth, and holding the keys of power. The Jews had to obey his instructions or be damned, by their own law; and Christ Himself fulfilled all righteousness in becoming obedient to the law which he had given to Moses on the mount, and thereby magnified it and made it honorable, instead of destroying it. The son of Zacharias wrested the keys, the kingdom, the power, the glory from the Jews, by the holy anointing and decree of heaven, and these three reasons constitute him the greatest prophet born of a woman." (*History of the Church* 5:260-61.)

The Restoration of the Aaronic Priesthood

On May 15, 1829, John the Baptist returned to the earth in response to a prayerful inquiry offered by Joseph Smith and Oliver Cowdery. Laying his hands upon these brethren, he conferred upon them the Aaronic Priesthood:

"Upon you my fellow servants, in the name of Messiah I confer the Priesthood of Aaron, which holds the keys of the ministering of angels, and of the gospel of repentance, and of baptism by immersion for the remission of sins; and this shall never be taken again from the earth, until the sons of Levi do offer again an offering unto the Lord in righteousness." (D&C 13.)

Oliver Cowdery wrote concerning these events:

After writing the account given of the Savior's ministry to the remnant of the seed of Jacob, upon this continent [Oliver had just finished transcribing the record known as the Book of Mormon], it was easy to be seen, as the prophet said would be, that darkness covered the earth and gross darkness the minds of the people. On reflecting further it was easy to be seen that amid the great strife and noise concerning religion, none had authority from God to administer the ordinances of the Gospel. For the question might be asked, have men authority to administer in the name of Christ, who deny revelations, when His testimony is no less than the spirit of prophecy, and His religion based, built, and sustained by immediate revelations, in all ages of the world when He has had a people on earth? If these facts were buried, and carefully concealed by men whose craft would have been in danger if once permitted to shine in the faces of men, they were no longer to us; and we only waited for the commandment to be given "Arise and be baptized."

This was not long desired before it was realized. The Lord, who is rich in mercy, and ever willing to answer the consistent prayer of the humble, after we had called Him in a fervent manner, aside from the abodes of men, condescended to manifest to us His will. On a sudden, as from the midst of eternity, the voice of the Redeemer spake peace to us. While the veil was parted and the angel of God came down clothed with glory, and delivered the anxiously looked for message, and the keys of the Gospel of repentance. What joy! what wonder! what amazement! While the world was racked and distracted—while millions were groping as the blind for the wall, and while all men were resting upon uncertainty, as a general mass, our eyes beheld, our ears heard, as in the "blaze of day"; yes, more—above the glitter of the May sunbeam, which then shed its brilliancy over the face of nature! Then his voice, though mild, pierced to the center, and his words, "I am thy fellow-servant," dispelled every fear. We listened, we gazed, we admired! 'Twas the voice of an angel, from glory, 'twas a message from the Most High! And as we heard we rejoiced, while His love enkindled upon our souls, and we were wrapped in the vision of the Almighty! Where was room for doubt? Nowhere; uncertainty had fled, doubt had sunk no more to rise, while fiction and deception had fled forever!

. . . what joy filled our hearts, and with what surprise we must have bowed, (for who would not have bowed the knee for such a blessing?) when we received under his hand the Holy Priesthood as he said, "Upon you my fellow servants, in the name of Messiah, I confer this Priesthood and this authority, which shall remain upon earth, that the Sons of Levi may yet offer an offering unto the Lord in righteousness!" (*Times and Seasons* 2:201.)

The Keys of the Aaronic Priesthood

The three keys associated with the Priesthood of Aaron—"the keys of the ministering of angels, and of the gospel of repentance, and of baptism by immersion for the remission of sins"—represent the essential elements necessary for holders of the preparatory priesthood to perform their duties.

1. In order to understand *the keys of the ministering of angels*, it is important to understand the nature and purpose of these heavenly beings. Elder Bruce R. McConkie defines angels as "God's messengers, those individuals whom he sends . . . to deliver his messages; to minister to his children; to teach them the doctrines of salvation; to call them to repentance; to give them priesthood and keys; to save them in perilous circumstances; to guide them in the performance of his work; to gather his elect in the last days; to perform all needful things relative to his work." (*Mormon Doctrine*, Bookcraft, 2nd ed., 1966, p. 35.)

Angels are chosen by the Lord. They are beings in various stages of their eternal progression and may include the following:

a. Premortal beings—righteous spirits who performed as angels in the spirit world in fighting against Satan and his angels. (Revelation 12:7.) When Adam and Eve were driven from the Garden of Eden, the Lord sent angels to minister unto them. (Moses 5:6-8.)

b. Translated beings, such as the three Nephite disciples, who experienced a change in their bodies and therefore did not suffer death, but who, when their mission is completed, shall be changed from mortality to immortality. (3 Nephi 28:37-38.)

c. Resurrected beings who lived and died upon this earth and have progressed farther than any other messengers of heaven. Included in this group are Peter, James, John the Baptist, and many other of the noble and great beings. These beings have resurrected bodies and will ultimately receive

their exaltation. They will then be gods and no longer ministering angels. (D&C 88:107.)

d. Spirits of loved ones who have been faithful and
worthy members of the Church and who may serve as the
Lord's angels to minister unto men. These are "the spirits of
just men made perfect, they who are not resurrected, but inherit the same glory" as those angels who have resurrected
bodies. (D&C 129.) President Joseph F. Smith said, "Our fathers and mothers, brothers, sisters and friends who have
passed away from this earth, having been faithful, and
worthy to enjoy these rights and privileges, may have a mission given them to visit their relatives and friends upon the
earth again, bringing from the divine Presence messages of
love, of warning, or reproof and instruction, to those whom
they had learned to love in the flesh." (*Gospel Doctrine*, p.
436.)

From the time of Adam to the present, angels have ministered to men whenever they have had sufficient faith.
When men fail to receive these ministrations, it is a sign of
their unbelief. Moroni states, "Have angels ceased to appear
unto the children of men? . . . Nay; . . . it is by faith that angels appear unto men; wherefore, if these things have ceased
wo be unto the children of men, for it is because of unbelief,
and all is vain." (Moroni 7:36-37.)

President Wilford Woodruff reported that he had several
dramatic ministrations from an angel of the Lord. On one
occasion when he held the office of a priest in the Aaronic
Priesthood, an angel appeared to him: "He (referring to the
angel) presented before me a panorama. He told me he wanted me to see with my eyes and understand with my mind
what was coming to pass in the earth before the coming of
the Son of Man. . . . Then he showed me the resurrection of
the dead—what is termed the first and second resurrection."
(*Millennial Star*, September 28, 1905, p. 612.)

President Woodruff made two other relevant points with
regard to the ministering of angels.

First, when one of the apostles commented that he had
prayed for a long time for the Lord to send an angel to minister to him, President Woodruff replied, "I told him that the

Lord never did and never will send an angel to anybody, merely to gratify the desire of the individual to see an angel. If the Lord sends an angel to anyone, he sends him to perform a work that can be performed only by the administration of an angel." (Ibid., p. 609.)

Second, President Woodruff commented regarding the relationship between the Holy Ghost as a witness and the ministration of an angel as a messenger:

"Now, I have always said, and I want to say it to you, that the Holy Ghost is what every Saint of God needs. It is far more important that a man should have this gift than he should have the administration of an angel, unless it is necessary for an angel to teach him something that he has not been taught." (Ibid., p. 610.)

"I have had the Holy Ghost in my travels. . . . I have referred to the administration of angels to myself. What did these angels do? One of them taught me some things relative to the signs that should precede the coming of the Son of Man. Others saved my life. What then? They turned and left me. But how is it with the Holy Ghost? The Holy Ghost does not leave me if I do my duty. It does not leave any man who does his duty." (Ibid., p. 638.)

Angels minister unto men and speak unto men through the power of the Holy Ghost. (2 Nephi 32:3.) Indeed, the ministry of angels is associated with the Aaronic Priesthood —to bring men to Christ through the gospel of faith unto repentance and baptism by immersion for the remission of sins.

2. The key of the "gospel of repentance" simply means that the authority and the responsibility to preach repentance from sin begin with the deacon, teacher, and priest, and they are directed by the ward bishopric, who hold the keys to this ministry. The actual gift of repentance is available to all who come unto the Lord with "a broken heart and a contrite spirit." (3 Nephi 9:20.)

John the Baptist represented the perfect example of the use of the gospel of repentance as he came out of the wilderness to cry repentance to all men. (Matthew 9:20.) Had John failed to preach repentance unto the Hebrews, he would have failed to exercise one of the great keys of the

Aaronic Priesthood and, therefore, would have been an imposter and not an Elias, or forerunner of the coming of the Lord. (Matthew 3:3.)

3. *Baptism for the remission of sins* was not a new ordinance of the gospel, but existed on the earth from the time of Adam. (Moses 6:64-65.) Enoch and Noah both taught their people concerning this ordinance. (Moses 7:10-11; 8:23-24.) The Nephites also practiced this ordinance, as evidenced by the baptisms performed by Alma at the Waters of Mormon. (Mosiah 18:13-16.)

When we are truly repentant for our past sins and are desirous of making a covenant with the Lord that we will continue steadfast in the faith, and "are desirous to come into the fold of God, and to be called his people, and are willing to bear one another's burdens, that they may be light; . . . and to stand as witnesses of God at all times and in all things, and in all places . . . even until death, . . . and be numbered with those of the first resurrection, that [we] may have eternal life," then we may receive the blessings that accrue as a result of baptism. (Mosiah 18:8-9.)

Only two of the four offices in the Aaronic Priesthood have the authority to baptize: a bishop and a priest. While the priest has the authority to baptize, he may exercise that authority only under the direction of the bishop or branch president, who holds the keys of that ordinance in his ward or branch. Although a priest may perform the ordinance of baptism, he does not have power to confer the Holy Ghost. John, in baptizing the repentant sinner with water, taught, "I indeed baptize you with water unto repentance: but he that cometh after me . . . shall baptize you with the Holy Ghost, and with fire." (Matthew 3:11.)

Duties of the Aaronic Priesthood

The duties of the Aaronic Priesthood are inseparably bound to the ministry of the Aaronic Priesthood. The duties performed by deacons, teachers, and priests today are no less an essential part of the ministry of the Aaronic Priesthood than those performed by holders of the priesthood at the time of Aaron or in Christ's early church.

The duties now performed by deacons, teachers, and priests are an essential part of the training associated with the preparatory priesthood. Preparatory for what? For receiving the greater or Melchizedek Priesthood, which holds the keys of exaltation in the celestial kingdom. Young men in the Church today should realize that every duty they perform as deacons, teachers, or priests has a spiritual purpose both in the form of administering the outward ordinances of the Church and in preparing young men for the responsibilities of the Melchizedek Priesthood. All blessings from the Lord come through faithfulness to duty and keeping the commandments; thus we may understand why, among other reasons, the Lord instituted the Aaronic Priesthood as a preparatory priesthood before a young man receives the Melchizedek Priesthood.

Each young man who receives the Aaronic Priesthood is "called of God, as was Aaron," to that priesthood; and as he takes his calling and magnifies it, he is entitled to the blessings of the Holy Spirit associated with that priesthood.

Duties of Deacons

The office of the deacon is one of the ordained offices of the Aaronic Priesthood. Although it is the first office in the Aaronic Priesthood, it is a significant and holy calling in the kingdom of God. Each person receives the Aaronic Priesthood before he is ordained the first time to an office in that priesthood. Thus the deacon receives as much priesthood as the priest, but he is limited in the use of that priesthood.

Deacons are involved in missionary work, for they are to "warn, expound, exhort, and teach, and invite all to come unto Christ." (D&C 20:59.) They are "appointed to watch over the church, to be standing ministers unto the church." (D&C 84:111.) In fulfilling this assignment, the deacon is at the call of the bishop to minister to the needs of ward members. He serves ward members in the following ways:

1. Collecting fast offerings, which assists the bishop in administering to the poor and needy of the Church.

2. Passing the sacrament, a highly sacred assignment that is at the center of our worship service.

3. Serving as a bishop's messenger.

4. Maintaining the physical facilities of the Church, caring for the grounds and buildings by making sure they are clean, orderly, and well cared for.

Deacons are authorized and obliged to assist the teacher in all his duties, if occasion requires. (D&C 20:57.) However, neither teachers nor deacons "have authority to baptize, administer the sacrament, or lay on hands." (D&C 20:58.)

Duties of Teachers

The office of teacher is also an ordained office of the Aaronic Priesthood. The teacher does not have any more priesthood than the deacon, but he does have the right to exercise more priesthood authority. A teacher exercises all the rights and authorities of a deacon and may, upon request, perform all the duties of a deacon.

The Lord gave the following description of the duties of the teacher: "The teacher's duty is to watch over the church always, and be with and strengthen them; and see that there is no iniquity in the church, neither hardness with each other, neither lying, backbiting, nor evil speaking; and see that the church meet together often, and also see that all the members do their duty. And he is to take the lead of meetings in the absence of the elder or priest." (D&C 20:53-56.) The teacher is to minister to the needs of the members. Home teaching is one of the ways in which he fulfills this duty.

The divine injunction to teach, which by definition accrues to the office of teacher, is yet another duty of this office. The teacher is to teach "the principles of my gospel, which are in the Bible and the Book of Mormon, in the which is the fulness of the gospel." (D&C 42:12.) In addition, he has a responsibility to do missionary work, to "invite all to come unto Christ." (D&C 20:59.)

The office of teacher carries with it a leadership responsibility. When there is no priest or elder present, he is "to take the lead of meetings." (D&C 20:56.)

Duties of Priests

The office of priest is the oldest office in the Aaronic Priesthood, having been given to Aaron and his sons by Moses upon direction of the Lord. (Exodus 28:1.) A priest may do all that a deacon or teacher can do, with some additional responsibilities and duties.

The Lord revealed the duties of a priest in his revelation on Church government:

"The priest's duty is to preach, teach, expound, exhort, and baptize, and administer the sacrament, and visit the house of each member, and exhort them to pray vocally and in secret and attend to all family duties.

"And he may also ordain other priests, teachers, and deacons. And he is to take the lead of meetings when there is no elder present;

"But when there is an elder present, he is only to preach, teach, expound, exhort, and baptize, and visit the house of each member, exhorting them to pray vocally and in secret and attend to all family duties.

"In all these duties the priest is to assist the elder if occasion requires." (D&C 20:46-52.)

The priest in the Aaronic Priesthood, as well as the teacher and deacon, has a responsibility to so order his life that he is able to have the Holy Spirit with him when he teaches. This requires the exercise of great faith: "And the Spirit shall be given unto you by the prayer of faith; and if ye receive not the Spirit ye shall not teach." (D&C 42:14.)

Priests may not be called on full-time missions as were the priests in the time of the Prophet Joseph Smith, but they may be called upon to serve as temporary companions to Melchizedek Priesthood holders serving as missionaries. Priests have the responsibility to teach not only by the spoken word, but also by their daily example.

The duty of baptizing is a divine commission given to priests. They are also commissioned to administer the sacrament, which is done in renewal of the baptismal covenant and as a remembrance of the atoning sacrifice of our Savior.

Another of the duties of the priest is to "visit the house of each member, and exhort them to pray vocally and in secret and attend to all family duties." (D&C 20:47.) He accomplishes this duty through home teaching, usually as a companion to a Melchizedek Priesthood bearer. Where no Melchizedek Priesthood bearer is available, the priest may perform this duty alone.

In his progress through the priesthood, a young man who holds the office of priest may, by assignment and authorization from the presiding officer who holds the keys in his ward or branch, lay his hands upon another's head and "ordain other priests, teachers, and deacons." (D&C 20:48.)

The priest may "take the lead of meetings where there is no elder present." While he may conduct a meeting by assignment, he may *preside* only when no Melchizedek Priesthood bearer is present. Even in the priests quorum the priest does not preside, for the bishop is president of the priests quorum, a responsibility that cannot be delegated. (D&C 107:87-88.)

A Vision of the Aaronic Priesthood

A few years ago Bishop Victor L. Brown, Presiding Bishop of the Church, retold the following experience in general conference, in the words of a young man who wrote:

At one time I attended a ward which had almost no Melchizedek Priesthood holders in it. But it was not in any way dulled in spirituality. On the contrary, many of its members witnessed the greatest display of priesthood power they had ever known.

"The power was centered in the priests. For the first time in their lives they were called upon to perform all the duties of the priests and administer to the needs of their fellow ward members. They were seriously called to home teach—not just to be a yawning appendage to an elder making a social call but to bless their brothers and sisters.

"Previous to this time I had been with four of these priests in a different situation. There I regarded them to be common hoodlums. They drove away every seminary teacher after two or three months. They spread havoc over the countryside on Scouting trips. *But when they were needed—when they were trusted with a vital mission—they were among those who shone the most brilliantly in priesthood service.*

"The secret was that the bishop called upon his Aaronic Priesthood to rise to the stature of men to whom angels might well appear; and they rose to that stature, administering relief to those who might be in want and strengthening those who needed strengthening. Not only were the other ward members built up but so were the members of the quorum themselves. A great unity spread throughout the ward and every member began to have a taste of what it is for a people to be of one mind and one heart. There was nothing inexplicable in all of this; it was just the proper exercise of the Aaronic Priesthood." (*Ensign*, November 1975, p. 68.)

When Aaronic Priesthood holders in their quorums fulfill their scriptural duties and responsibilities, the Aaronic Priesthood becomes a vital and powerful force for preparing them to carry forth the gospel unto the ends of the earth. The Church will see double, even triple, the number of missionaries prepared to carry the gospel message. And as they take responsibilities to serve in leadership capacities through their quorums, how great will be their influence for good in the wards and stakes in which they will later serve as bishops, stake presidents, Scoutmasters, teachers and advisers, and in other leadership capacities. The righteousness of the young men of the Aaronic Priesthood will be felt throughout the world, and indeed the sons of Levi will be ready to offer up an offering in righteousness to the Lord!

THE
QUORUM

Elder Boyd K. Packer

In ancient days when a man was appointed to a select body, his commission, always written in Latin, outlined the responsibility of the organization, defined who should be members, and then invariably contained the words "*quorum vos unum*," meaning "of whom we will that you be one."

The word *quorum*, which does not appear in either the Old Testament or the New Testament, from that beginning came to mean that select group without whose consent business could not be transacted, nor work proceed with authority. In the dispensation of the fulness of times, the Lord instructed that the priesthood should be organized into quorums, meaning selected assemblies of brethren given authority that his business might be transacted and his work proceed.

The word *quorum* is so recognized in *Webster's Dictionary* as "a Mormon body comprising those in the same grade of priesthood."

The government of the Lord's affairs in this dispensation rests in The Church of Jesus Christ of Latter-day Saints, which by his own declaration is "the only true and living church upon the face of the whole earth, with which I, the Lord, am well pleased, speaking unto the church collectively and not individually." (D&C 1:30.)

The priesthood, which is always associated with God's work, "continueth in the church of God in all generations, and is without beginning of days or end of years." (D&C 84:17.)

It continues in our day. Men, young and old, are called out of the world and received into the Church by baptism. With limitations and standards of worthiness established by the Lord, men may qualify by making themselves worthy for ordination into that comparatively small body of men on this earth who are commissioned to hold authority and transact the business of the Lord at this time.

The Melchizedek Priesthood

"There are, in the church, two priesthoods, namely, the Melchizedek and the Aaronic, including the Levitical Priesthood.

"Why the first is called the Melchizedek Priesthood is because Melchizedek was such a great high priest.

"Before his day it was called *the Holy Priesthood, after the Order of the Son of God.*

"But out of respect or reverence to the name of the Supreme Being, to avoid the too frequent repetition of his name, they, the church, in ancient days, called that priesthood after Melchizedek, or the Melchizedek Priesthood." (D&C 107:1-4.)

"The Melchizedek Priesthood holds the right of presidency, and has power and authority over all the offices in the church in all ages of the world, to administer in spiritual things." (D&C 107:8.)

"All other authorities or offices in the church are appendages to this priesthood." (D&C 107:5.)

"And this greater priesthood administereth the gospel and holdeth the key of the mysteries of the kingdom, even the key of the knowledge of God.

"Therefore, in the ordinances thereof, the power of godliness is manifest.

"And without the ordinances thereof, and the authority of the priesthood, the power of godliness is not manifest unto men in the flesh." (D&C 84:19-21.)

There are in the greater priesthood these offices:

1. The *elder*, who is a standing home minister.

2. The *seventy*, who is a traveling minister.

3. The *high priest*, who is to administer in spiritual things and to preside as his calling in the Church requires.

4. The *patriarch*, who seals blessings upon the members of the Church.

5. The *apostle*, who is a traveling councilor and a special witness of the name of Christ in all the world.

6. The *presidency of the high priesthood*, who have the right to officiate in all the offices of the priesthood. (See *A Guide for Quorums of the Melchizedek Priesthood*, Council of the Twelve, 1930, p. 13.)

There are five quorums mentioned in the Doctrine and Covenants relating to the greater priesthood. They are:

1. The *quorums of elders*, "which quorum is instituted for standing ministers; nevertheless they may travel, yet they are ordained to be standing ministers." (D&C 124:137.) A full quorum consists of ninety-six elders, presided over by a quorum presidency called by the president of the stake. Those brethren now designated as prospective elders affiliate with the quorums of elders.

2. The *quorums of seventy*, "which quorum is instituted for traveling elders to bear record of my name in all the world." (D&C 124:139.) This quorum numbers seventy brethren, presided over by seven presidents called by the stake president after conferring with the First Quorum of the Seventy. Their assignment is missionary work, in which they receive some guidance from the First Quorum of the Seventy.

3. The *quorums of high priests*, each with a membership of all high priests residing within the boundaries of a stake, including patriarchs and bishops. The stake president and his counselors form the presidency of this quorum.

4. The *Quorum of the Twelve Apostles*, made up of those men ordained as apostles and sustained as members of that quorum. (D&C 107:23-24.)

5. The *quorum of the First Presidency* of the Church, consisting of the president and his two counselors. (D&C 107:22.)

The Aaronic Priesthood

"The second priesthood is called the Priesthood of Aaron, because it was conferred upon Aaron and his seed, throughout all their generations." (D&C 107:13.)

This priesthood "holds the keys of the ministering of angels, and of the gospel of repentance, and of baptism by immersion for the remission of sins." (D&C 13:1.)

"Why it is called the lesser priesthood is because it is an appendage to the greater, or the Melchizedek Priesthood, and has power in administering outward ordinances." (D&C 107:14.)

There are four offices in the Aaronic Priesthood:

1. The *deacon*, who is to "watch over the church," and to be a standing minister to the church. (D&C 84:111. See also D&C 20:57-59.)

2. The *teacher*, who is to "watch over the church always, and be with and strengthen them." (D&C 20:53.)

3. The *priest*, who is to "preach, teach, expound, exhort, and baptize, and administer the sacrament, And visit the house of each member." (D&C 20:46-47.)

4. The *bishop*, who presides over the Aaronic Priesthood and "administers in all temporal things." (D&C 107:68, 71.)

There are three quorums of the Aaronic Priesthood:

1. The *deacons quorum*, to consist of twelve deacons (D&C 107:85), with a presidency called by the bishop from among their members.

2. The *teachers quorum*, to number twenty-four members (D&C 107:86), with a presidency called by the bishop from among their numbers.

3. The *priests quorum*, to number forty-eight priests (D&C 107:87), presided over by the bishop of the ward to which the quorum belongs. (D&C 107:88.)

The bishop is a high priest and belongs to the high priests quorum.

In both priesthoods, a majority of the required number may constitute a quorum. When the number specified for a quorum is exceeded, the quorum may be—and perhaps generally should be—divided.

It is intended that every holder of the priesthood have membership in a quorum. It is a sacred privilege that comes with the bestowal of the priesthood. Priesthood and quorum membership are virtually synonymous.

In some cases a man may be ordained in an area where there are insufficient brethren to constitute a quorum. He has his priesthood file leader, and his channel of authority leads, as with those who belong to quorums, to the prophet and president of the Church.

When a young man reaches the age of twelve, he has conferred upon him the Aaronic Priesthood and is ordained to the office of deacon. Automatically, immediately, he becomes a member of a deacons quorum. From then on through life, it is contemplated that he will hold membership in a quorum of the priesthood.

Quorum membership is not optional. A man may not present himself to be ordained to an office in the priesthood and yet choose at once not to belong to a quorum, or choose to affiliate with a quorum made up of brethren holding a different office in the priesthood. He is a member of the appropriate quorum, and by his actions he either sustains or degrades it. He maintains his membership in the quorum until he is ordained to another office in the priesthood and automatically becomes a member of another quorum. If he moves from the area of his quorum, he is at once eligible for membership in the appropriate quorum in the area where his church membership is located.

A man who becomes inactive does not lose his membership in the quorum. He may lose interest in the quorum, but the quorum must never lose interest in him. The quorum is responsible always and continually for each of its members. To ignore an inactive member, to withdraw interest in and contact with him, is an abrogation of his rights as a holder of the priesthood. He cannot be denied membership or participation in a quorum except by proper court action. A man guilty of transgression is subject to disciplinary action. He may be disfellowshipped, in which case sanctions are employed that prevent him from exercising his priesthood until repentance has been completed and those privileges restored. If he is excommunicated from the Church, he no longer holds the priesthood nor membership in a quorum.

If a quorum member is guilty of transgression, to fail to take proper disciplinary action when it is warranted is to offend the privileges of that man. Each of us should have the right to proper discipline. Discipline is an expression of love.

In the priesthood, it may become an exalted expression of love, for the word "discipline" comes from the word "disciple."

If his priesthood quorum functions properly, it is almost impossible for a man sustained by the brethren of his quorum to fail in any phase of life's responsibility.

I repeat, all other authorities or offices in the Church are appendages to the higher priesthood.

A worthy priesthood holder may be called as an ecclesiastical officer in the Church, such as stake president, high councilor, or bishop, or be called as an officer, teacher or board member in an appendage organization, without altering his status as a member of the quorum. Such service neither enlarges nor can it diminish his membership in a quorum.

Though he may be called to and released from such assignments, his membership in his quorum is a steady, sustaining citizenship that becomes his right as a holder of the priesthood. And the holding of the priesthood, including the attendant membership in the quorum, ought to be regarded as a sacred privilege.

To be called to preside over a quorum, to be called as the secretary of a quorum, or to be called to any other assignment to sustain the quorum, is in and of itself a signal spiritual honor. It is likewise a monumental responsibility.

Each person who holds the priesthood ought to energetically determine to maintain his standards in order to be worthy of such membership. Priorities in his thinking ought to be so arranged that he regards the priesthood he holds, from which all other offices and authorities must draw their power, as having preference and priority in his feelings and his attentions.

I can easily think of our Sunday School, for instance, as a priesthood Sunday School. It is presided over by a Sunday School president who is a holder of the priesthood and is himself a member of a quorum. His calling, which is relatively temporary, is an honorable service that he renders for a time and a season. He is a credit to his quorum in rendering it. He will, of course, one day be released from it, but it is not contemplated that he will spend a day on this earth without being a member of a quorum.

When a priesthood holder is called to a position in an appendage organization, he is representing his quorum in that sacred responsibility. He is not taken away from his quorum to fulfill the assignment.

These appendant services round out a fullness of life and provide members of the quorums and their families a fullness of experience, activity, and training. They are, in a very real sense, priesthood functions and activities.

Such callings in the Church are important and ought so to be esteemed. Their relative importance, however, does not and must not give them presumed ascendency over those offices in the priesthood and those callings to govern the quorums of the priesthood. The priesthood is the source of all strength and authority for all organizations and offices in the Church.

One can become careless with his quorum membership. Just as membership in a family or patriotism toward one's country may weaken and fail, so may quorum membership if it is taken for granted. In our day there is an urgent need for every single holder of the priesthood to bolster his spiritual patriotism or allegiance to his quorum.

Stake presidents cannot devote their time and attention to those organizations which are appended to the priesthood to the neglect of the priesthood and the quorums of the priesthood, and succeed in establishing godliness among our people.

They cannot fund those appended organizations with a disproportionate amount of time, or of talent, or of funds, and succeed in bringing godliness to the people.

The strength in the quorum is the key to the strength of the stake. The quorum will be as strong as the individual member. We all have the obligation and responsibility to honor our priesthood, to be worthy citizens of the priesthood quorum.

"For whoso is faithful unto the obtaining these two priesthoods of which I have spoken, and the magnifying their calling, are sanctified by the Spirit unto the renewing of their bodies.

"They become the sons of Moses and of Aaron and the seed of Abraham, and the church and kingdom, and the elect of God.

"And also all they who receive this priesthood receive me, saith the Lord;

"For he that receiveth my servants receiveth me;

"And he that receiveth me receiveth my Father;

"And he that receiveth my Father receiveth my Father's kingdom; therefore all that my Father hath shall be given unto him.

"And this is according to the oath and covenant which belongeth to the priesthood.

"Therefore, all those who receive the priesthood, receive this oath and covenant of my Father, which he cannot break, neither can it be moved." (D&C 84:33-40.)

God grant that all of us who hold the priesthood and each of us who is a member of a quorum will honor that priesthood, will sustain that quorum, to the end that godliness may be found in the lives of all Latter-day Saints.

TO TEACH,
TO TESTIFY,
TO BE TRUE

Elder Marvin J. Ashton

The history of the Church, both ancient and modern, highlights many great priesthood holders who have set examples to show us the importance of keeping the oath and covenant of the priesthood, and to show us how to magnify our callings and responsibilities in the priesthood.

The greatest example of priesthood leadership in the Lord's church, however, is the Savior himself. By example, he teaches us three great priesthood responsibilities, as described in the eighth chapter of John. These three principles and responsibilities are (1) to teach, (2) to testify, and (3) to be true.

1. To Teach
"Jesus went unto the mount of Olives.

"And early in the morning he came again into the temple, and all the people came unto him; and he sat down, and taught them." (John 8:1-2.)

These two verses give us as priesthood holders a profound insight into Jesus' way of life and the way in which he taught. His going to the Mount of Olives was for preparation. He didn't go there for the scenery. He went for the seclusion that would make possible purposeful meditation, contemplation, solitude, prayer, pondering, privacy, pleading, and spiritual refreshment. He went early to prepare himself for the day. He went to commune with his Father in humble supplication. His way of living was natural, humble, and selfless. He lived to do the will of his Father.

In his preparations to teach and to magnify his calling, he showed the importance of self-management and self-discipline. How meaningful are the two words "Jesus went." He wasn't carried. He wasn't commanded. On his own, through proper self-motivation, he went. How grateful those of us who follow him should be for the powerful description "Jesus went"!

"And early in the day he came again." We learn from these choice words the importance of using the early part of the morning to start and proceed. In modern revelation the Lord tells us, "Cease to sleep longer than is needful; retire to thy bed early, that ye may not be weary; arise early, that your bodies and your minds may be invigorated." (D&C 88:124.) The Savior set the example for this wise counsel.

John tells us that not only did he come early in the day, but "he came again." Once is not enough. He was in the habit of going into the temple or church on a continuing basis to converse, share, teach, and learn. Is it any wonder that those who listened and mingled were astonished at his wisdom and understanding? Again, in our day we are taught: "See that the church meet together often, and also see that all the members do their duty. . . . It is expedient that the church meet together often to partake of bread and wine in the remembrance of the Lord Jesus." (D&C 20:55, 75.) "And that thou mayest more fully keep thyself unspotted from the world, thou shalt go to the house of prayer and offer up thy sacraments upon my holy day." (D&C 59:9.) Just as Jesus "came again," we also must constantly renew our covenants with the Lord.

"He sat down and taught them." He didn't talk down. He communicated on the people's level, eye to eye, in understandable parables and persuasion. He didn't threaten, boast, or ridicule. He taught as one who was in tune and approachable. He never let problems or discouragement overcome the positive appeal and approach that were his divine teaching tools. His effect on the world as a teacher speaks for itself as to his strength in human relationships.

All of us should take strength and comfort from the fact that even though "all the people came unto him," he didn't convert them all. He kept trying—teaching and leading in a meaningful way. Some who came were skeptics, enemies, accusers, traitors, and doubters; others were honest in heart

—children, aged, blind, deaf, lame, sick, learned, and friends. He taught them all in equal love.

How can we as priesthood bearers use these great teaching principles? We can "go to the mount" through the scriptures. The Lord has told us in our day: "The Book of Mormon and the holy scriptures are given for your instruction." (D&C 33:16.) "I give unto you a commandment that . . . ye shall teach them [the scriptures] unto all men; for they shall be taught unto all nations, kindreds, tongues and people." (D&C 42:58.) We can prepare to teach through personal commitment, meditation, pondering, and contemplation. We can learn the value of individual and group prayers. We can learn to teach on the level of the listener, and to be wise and prudent in our approach. Above all, we can learn the worth of teaching by personal example.

Verses 3 to 11 in John 8 show us well how the Savior taught:

"And the scribes and Pharisees brought unto him a woman taken in adultery; and when they had set her in the midst, they say unto him, Master, this woman was taken in adultery, in the very act. Now Moses in the law commanded us, that such should be stoned: but what sayest thou?

"This they said, tempting him, that they might have to accuse him. But Jesus stooped down, and with his finger wrote on the ground, as though he heard them not.

"So when they continued asking him, he lifted up himself, and said unto them, He that is without sin among you, let him first cast a stone at her. And again he stooped down and wrote on the ground.

"And they which heard it, being convicted by their own conscience, went out one by one, beginning at the eldest, even unto the last: and Jesus was left alone, and the woman standing in the midst.

"When Jesus had lifted up himself, and saw none but the woman, he said unto her, Woman, where are those thine accusers? hath no man condemned thee? She said, No man, Lord. And Jesus said unto her, Neither do I condemn thee: go, and sin no more."

By example, in unsurpassing love and compassion, the Savior taught his disciples—and us.

2. To Testify

"He that sent me is true. . . . And he that sent me is with me." (John 8:26, 29.)

When we testify, we teach and we share our witness, just as Jesus, the Son of God, taught and bore witness of the Father. In the great revelation on priesthood, section 84 of the Doctrine and Covenants, the Lord reiterates this principle: "Therefore, go ye into all the world; and unto whatsoever place ye cannot go ye shall send, that the testimony may go from you into all the world." (D&C 84:62.) As priesthood bearers, we can magnify our callings and keep the oath and covenant we have made by bearing witness in word and in deed.

In John 8:12-18 the Savior bore a powerful testimony of himself and his mission. Even though the Pharisees were there to ridicule, question, and scorn, he could not be backed away from the truth about himself.

"Then spake Jesus again unto them, saying, I am the light of the world: he that followeth me shall not walk in darkness, but shall have the light of life.

"The Pharisees therefore said unto him, Thou bearest record of thyself; thy record is not true.

"Jesus answered and said unto them, Though I bear record of myself, yet my record is true: for I know whence I came, and whither I go; but ye cannot tell whence I come, and whither I go.

"Ye judge after the flesh; I judge no man. And yet if I judge, my judgment is true: for I am not alone, but I and the Father that sent me.

"It is also written in your law, that the testimony of two men is true. I am one that bear witness of myself, and the Father that sent me beareth witness of me."

This powerful testimony concluded with Jesus' knowledge that he was not alone, that his judgment was true, and that his Father's witness joined his own.

There are two types of testimonies. We are all entitled to one or the other. The first might be called a sudden impact testimony—that of a convert, or of an inactive member who feels the Spirit move for the first time.

In a special seminar held in one of our stakes to reactivate prospective elders, a patient and good instructor had taught the lessons but felt he was having little success. After fasting and prayer to seek guidance in what he could do to help the men in the class gain the priesthood and become temple-worthy, he decided to hold a testimony meeting. With some anxiety he approached the prospective elders and told them he would like to share with them his testimony of the Savior and of the latter-day work that blessed his life.

When he concluded his own testimony, he invited the others to share any simple belief, any stirring of the Spirit that might be in their hearts. There followed that long, sometimes welcome, sometimes awkward, silence that precedes the bearing of testimonies. Each second seemed extremely long, but finally a man in his mid-fifties stood. He was a successful man, articulate and well groomed. In halting words he said simply, "The weight of the truth of what you have said is more than I can know and still remain silent. I know that what you say is true. I believe in the Savior and in Joseph Smith. I want to hold the priesthood!"

The spirit in the room was overpowering. That one simple testimony converted eleven of the twelve men present. Those conversions came because one man who had been away felt the sudden impact of the Spirit, and because a loving teacher cared and bore his own quiet testimony.

The second type of testimony is a quiet testimony, one that we grow up with, one that we have always had. It too is real. It grows through obedience, service, and sharing. It is like the testimony of our prophet Spencer W. Kimball when he says, "My brethren and sisters, I testify to you that this is the Lord's work and that it is true. We are on the Lord's errand. This is His church and He is its head and the chief cornerstone. God lives, and Jesus is the Christ. He is the Only Begotten Son, the Savior and Redeemer of this world. I leave you with this testimony and with my blessings and my love and affection, in the name of Jesus Christ. Amen." (*Ensign*, May 1981, p. 79.)

Both types of testimony are true and worthy. Be pleased to have one or the other. Perhaps you are lucky enough to have experienced some of both. Testimonies grow as they are nurtured, and they stay strong as we keep the commandments and pursue proper personal conduct.

3. To Be True

As holders of the holy priesthood, we must be true to correct principles. We have a responsibility to continue faithfully in being true to the gospel. We cannot take a rest or vacation from these principles. We will be judged according to our ability and strength in continuing in His word.

How can we tell if we are being true, worthy disciples?

"Then said Jesus to those Jews which believed on him, If ye continue in my word, then are ye my disciples indeed; and ye shall know the truth, and the truth shall make you free.

"They answered him, We be Abraham's seed, and were never in bondage to any man: how sayest thou, Ye shall be made free?

"Jesus answered them, Verily, verily, I say unto you, Whosoever committeth sin is the servant of sin. And the servant abideth not in the house for ever: but the Son abideth ever.

"If the Son therefore shall make you free, ye shall be free indeed." (John 8:31-36.)

Being true to our principles, if they are correct principles, can bring a kind of freedom and self-esteem that can be gained no other way.

Recently I was told of a young man who had been awarded a scholarship worth several thousand dollars. There was some question as to whether the young man could accept the scholarship and still fulfill his mission. In a letter to the university, he said, "I appreciate receiving the scholarship and hope that you will allow me to renew the scholarship when I return from a mission for my church. Perhaps I could be persuaded not to enter this fall if you think that would be best. However, I cannot be dissuaded from serving a mission for my church."

It matters little what the outcome of the situation will be for this young man. He was true to his calling, true to his responsibility, true to his priesthood. Being true involves much sacrifice—much heart, might, mind, and strength. If we are obedient to priesthood leaders, priesthood principles, and priesthood responsibilities, we will find ourselves being obedient and true to ourselves.

"Then spake Jesus again unto them, saying, I am the light of the world; he that followeth me shall not walk in darkness, but shall have the light of life." (John 8:12.)

President Kimball is an excellent example of one who has the light of life, one who is true. He continues. He climbs every mountain. He has walked through every valley. He does not falter. He does not quit. He just keeps going. In the opening session of general conference in April 1981, President Kimball outlined for us his past few busy and challenging months. He has traveled the world as ambassador for the gospel. He has been a tireless servant and tool in the hands of the Lord. He teaches, he testifies, and he is true. He continues with enthusiasm. He is true to God and to himself.

The Savior has taught us the rewards for being true. He has said: "Verily, verily, I say unto you, If a man keep my saying, he shall never see death." (John 8:51.) Each of us must resolve to be true, to be faithful, to be worthy of the trust placed in us. God will help us. We and God are a majority, and we can be victorious in all of life's challenges if we will continue in his strength.

God lives. Jesus is the Christ, our Redeemer. This is his church. Spencer W. Kimball is a prophet of God. God loves us. He wants us to be successful. We must not be weary in well-doing. We must teach, testify, and be true. And if we do so, he has promised that our "hearts might be comforted, being knit together, and unto all riches of the full assurance of understanding, to the acknowledgement of the mystery of God, and of the Father, and of Christ; in whom are hid all the treasures of wisdom and knowledge." (Colossians 2:2-3.)

PRIESTHOOD ORDINANCES

Elder Vaughn J. Featherstone

In an act of unselfish love, the Savior "riseth from supper, and laid aside his garments; and took a towel, and girded himself. After that he poureth water into a bason, and began to wash the disciples' feet, and to wipe them with the towel wherewith he was girded." (John 13:4-5.)

We, as members of the Lord's true church, understand and know that this sweet act of servitude and humility is an ordinance.

In John we also read the Savior's instructions to his disciples regarding this ordinance: "So after he had washed their feet, and had taken his garments, and was set down again, he said unto them, Know ye what I have done to you? Ye call me Master and Lord: And ye say well; for so I am. If I then, your Lord and Master, have washed your feet; ye also ought to wash one another's feet. For I have given you an example, that ye should do as I have done to you." (John 13:12-15.)

In this dispensation the Lord has reaffirmed the importance of this sacred special ordinance and has given instructions pertaining to it: "And ye shall not receive any among you into this school [of the prophets] save he is clean from the blood of this generation; And he shall be received by the ordinance of the washing of feet, for unto this end was the ordinance of the washing of feet instituted. And again, the ordinance of washing feet is to be administered by the president, or presiding elder of the church. It is to be commenced with prayer; and after partaking of bread and wine, he is to give himself according to the pattern given in the thirteenth chapter of John's testimony concerning me." (D&C 88:138-41.)

It seems appropriate to discuss this ordinance, as we lead into this chapter, to remind us again of the great, sacred nature of ordinances in the Church. As we ponder why there are ordinances in the Church, we consider many things. Those of us who are called to perform priesthood ordinances discover quickly that we function to bless others. The Savior, kneeling at the feet of his disciples and bathing their feet, portrays in the mind absolute charity, his pure love for his brethren. We picture the Savior of the world washing the dust and dirt from the disciples' feet. We can hardly imagine a more humbling, menial task. Even the most humble beggar in the street would be offended if he were asked to wash another's feet. Yet he whose work this is reaches to the greatest height of leadership and love by performing this act.

So, likewise, the Prophet Joseph was taught by the Master how to perform this ordinance. This higher ordinance is practiced in the Church. Little else can be discussed, it is so sacred, but it does give us a feeling for the other ordinances practiced in the divine church. Again, remember our priesthood and the ordinances are used to bless the lives of others. We can never bless ourselves or perform ordinances and officiate to bless ourselves. We perform ordinances and functions in the priesthood to bless all of humanity. The servant is truly greatest in the kingdom.

It has been my experience over the years to study and train employees, Church members, and youth in leadership principles. The term *leadership* is not used in the scriptures. Instructions and directions to the leader can be found under service, teaching, acts, example, and love, but not under leadership. Hence, ordinances give us an opportunity to serve our fellowmen in a Christlike way using the "priesthood after the order of the Son of God."

An ordinance as defined in Webster's dictionary is "an authoritative decree or direction; something ordained or decreed by fate or a deity; a prescribed usage, practice, or ceremony." With modern revelation we have added insight to the need for ordinances. Ordinances performed in the Church are by divine decree and must be fulfilled with exactness, order, and by those who are pure in heart, free from transgression, and authorized to so officiate. Every ordinance in the Church should be performed in a sacred, reverential attitude of service and obedience. Thus, this chapter deals with priesthood ordinances and the responsibility of the officiator and those being blessed through the ordinance. Some ordinances can be performed by virtue of ordination to the Melchizedek Priesthood. We need not seek permission or additional authority to administer to the sick. Other ordinances such as sealings in the temple must be authorized and additional powers and authority given by the laying on of hands by the prophet or one of his counselors, or a member of the Council of the Twelve to whom he delegates this responsibility.

Baptism is an ordinance about which much has been said. It is an essential ordinance and must be performed by those in authority, else the atonement of Jesus is of little effect in our lives. True, we can be resurrected and receive salvation, but there can be no exaltation or forgiveness of transgression except through baptism. Those who are baptized make sacred covenants with the Lord. Thus, proper preparation and understanding are vital. Section 20 of the Doctrine and Covenants sheds light on the attitude that one who is to be baptized should have:

"All those who humble themselves before God, and desire to be baptized, and come forth with broken hearts and contrite spirits, and witness before the church that they have truly repented of all their sins, and are willing to take upon them the name of Jesus Christ, having a determination to serve him to the end, and truly manifest by their words that they have received of the Spirit of Christ unto the remission of their sins, shall be received by baptism into his church." (D&C 20:37.)

We find in Mosiah qualifications of those to be baptized:

"And it came to pass that he said unto them: Behold, here are the waters of Mormon (for thus were they called) and now, as ye are desirous to come into the fold of God, and to be called his people, and are willing to bear one another's burdens, that they may be light;

"Yea, and are willing to mourn with those that mourn; yea, and comfort those that stand in need of comfort, and to stand as witnesses of God at all times and in all things, and in all places that ye may be in, even until death, that ye may be redeemed of God, and be numbered with those of the first resurrection, that ye may have eternal life." (Mosiah 18:8-9.)

We all understand these things. What we may not understand is that baptism should never be taken lightly nor discussed in a light-minded way. I remember a former Methodist minister in Texas who was truly converted. Some time after his baptism, which was years ago, he heard the missionaries in the mission office referring to baptism as dipping or dunking. He said that when he thought how much his baptism had meant to him, he wept to think they would discuss such a sacred ordinance in such a light-minded way.

Every baptismal service should be conducted with dignity and reverence. It seems appropriate that sacred music should be a prelude to the service. A beautiful tablecloth might grace the table (if held in the Relief Society room) with a lovely table decoration or centerpiece. The speakers should speak with the Spirit, and all who attend ought to understand that those who are being baptized are receiving the very fundamental and key ordinance that unlocks the door to the latter-day and temple ordinances. Many members have had special spiritual experiences and manifestations at the time of their baptism. Whether it happens or not isn't important. What is important is that our garments are washed clean through the blood of the Lamb and are no longer soiled. Isaiah said: "Come now, and let us reason together, saith the Lord: though your sins be as scarlet, they shall be as white as snow; though they be red like crimson, they shall be as wool." (Isaiah 1:18.)

Symbolically, baptism represents death, burial, and the resurrection: the death of the man of sin, buried in the waters of baptism, and coming forth spotless, having been cleansed. The entire baptismal service and ordinance is of such significant and eternal consequence that it must be approached with dignity, sincerity, humility, and gratitude. Oh, how we should love him who has provided the way whereby every soul who has lived, does now live, or will live, through faith, repentance, baptism, and endurance, can eventually gain the prize of eternal life.

The first principles and ordinances of the gospel are faith and repentance, baptism, and the gift of the Holy Ghost. The gift of the Holy Ghost transcends all knowledge, wisdom, and intellectual capacity. Moroni said, "And by the power of the Holy Ghost ye may know the truth of *all* things." (Moroni 10:5. Italics added.) Every member of the Church receives the gift as a promise predicated upon faithfulness in keeping the commandments. The Holy Ghost functions in our lives on a constant basis as we live worthily. He enlightens us at school, at work, in the business world, in our profession, in counseling our children, in decisions about our families, yea, about *all* things.

When the Savior visited the people on the American continent, they prayed. Third Nephi, chapter 19, states what they prayed for:

"And they did pray for that which they most desired; and they desired that the Holy Ghost should be given unto them. And when they had thus prayed they went down unto the water's edge, and the multitude followed them. And it came to pass that Nephi went down into the water and was baptized. And he baptized all those whom Jesus had chosen. And it came to pass when they were all baptized and had come up out of the water, the Holy Ghost did fall upon them, and they were filled with the Holy Ghost and with fire." (3 Nephi 19:9-13.)

The Savior prayed also. In the same chapter of Third Nephi we read his prayer: "Father, I thank thee that thou hast given the Holy Ghost unto these whom I have chosen; and it is because of their belief in me that I have chosen them out of the world. Father, I pray thee that thou wilt give the Holy Ghost unto all them that shall believe in their words. Father, thou hast given them the Holy Ghost because they believe in me; and thou seest that they believe in me because thou hearest them, and they pray unto me; and they pray unto me because I am with them." (3 Nephi 19:20-22.)

Then, we are told, "when Jesus had thus prayed unto the Father, he came unto his disciples, and behold, they did still continue, without ceasing, to pray unto him; and they did not multiply many words, *for it was given unto them what they should pray*, and they were filled with desire." (3 Nephi 19:24. Italics added.)

Those who have the gift of the Holy Ghost and live Christ-like lives "have no more disposition to do evil, but to do good continually." (Mosiah 5:2.) There is a reason baptism and the Holy Ghost are the first ordinances. When we are washed clean through the blood of the Lamb by our baptism and receive the gift of the Holy Ghost, our sins are removed and we are entitled to the constant companionship of the Holy Ghost, which will help us to know all things. It takes fine tuning of our lives before we hear "the still, small voice." It is always there, but we must be in tune on the right frequency to pick it up.

The sacrament is an ordinance that directly relates to our baptism and the atonement. When we partake of the sacrament, we renew the covenants that we made at baptism. Through constant repentance and covenants renewed, we can be forgiven from week to week, always understanding that repentance is necessary. The sacrament is a constant reminder that Jesus Christ atoned for our sins, that through his mercy and his willingness to satisfy the demands of justice we are his, paid for with a price. The sacrament takes on more sacred meaning when we realize this ordinance is inseparably connected to the atonement.

The priesthood officiators—deacons, teachers, and priests—should be appropriately attired. They should have clean—morally and physically—hands and hearts. They should feel that it is a holy privilege to officiate in any way. It would be wonderful if every deacon, teacher, and priest could attend a temple meeting or solemn assembly and officiate in the sacrament ordinance. Attitudes would change dramatically.

Because the ordinances of baptism and the sacrament are so closely related, the following story may appropriately be told here:

In a southern community during the depression, a teacher was hired for the one-room, one-class school. There were students from seven to fourteen years of age in the class. They ranged from the second grade to the eighth grade level. That year the students had driven four teachers out of the class. The school board asked the new teacher to sign a contract to assure his staying until the end of the year. He said, "I do not need to sign the contract. I will stay." The leaders suggested that the other teachers had all agreed to stay also, but had not completed the year, so they put pressure on him to sign the contract. He said, "Of course I will sign, because I intend to stay." He signed the contract.

The first day in class he stood before the students. They measured him, and he measured them. Finally he broke the silence and said, "I am your new teacher. I am going to stay until the end of the year. If we are going to have a good learning experience in this class it will be necessary to have some rules. What do you think the rules of conduct should be for this class?"

It was very quiet and then one student said, "Well, you shouldn't talk in class." He wrote, "no talking" on the chalkboard. "What other rules?" he said. Someone else suggested that the students should arrive on time. He wrote "punctuality" on the chalkboard as the second rule. Someone else suggested that there should be a rule against cheating. He wrote it down. After a few minutes they had thirteen or fourteen different rules of conduct for the class.

Then the teacher said, "Rules are of no value unless you live them. We ought to affix a punishment to each rule for whenever it is broken. How many lashes (with the small switch) for each of the rules?" Someone commented that punctuality was not all that serious because it only affected the one who was late. About two lashes ought to be enough. The teacher wrote down two lashes by the side of punctuality. "What about talking in class?" "Well," one student said, "that is more serious because it disrupts the whole class. How about seven lashes?" The teacher wrote down seven lashes as the punishment for talking in class. "What about cheating?" They all felt that was about the worst thing they could do and that cheating deserved the maximum punishment of ten lashes. For each of the thirteen or fourteen rules they decided upon a "just" punishment.

The teacher said, "We have listed the rules down this side of the board and we have determined a punishment for the violation of each rule and have listed that in this column. Now rules are not worth much even if you have a prescribed punishment unless you have an enforcer to enforce the rules. I can administer the punishment, but you must elect someone from this class to be the enforcer." The students quickly looked around the room and saw the class "bully" who was almost fourteen, oversized, pushed the younger kids around, and was probably the toughest kid in class. He was elected. Now they had rules, punishment, and an enforcer.

Everything went well for the first few days. Then one of the seven-year-old boys leaned over and started talking with his neighbor. The bully jumped from his seat, went down the aisle, picked the young boy up by his shoulders, carried him down the aisle, and planted him right in front of the teacher. Then he returned to his seat.

The teacher asked the boy if he was there the day they decided what the rules of conduct should be. With tears in his eyes, the boy nodded that he had. "And you agreed with the punishment if the rules were broken?" "Yes, sir," and the tears came more quickly. "Then take off your coat and receive the seven lashes." The tears came down faster and the little boy said, "Please, sir, don't make me do that." The teacher said, "Everyone in the class is waiting to see if I punish you for breaking the rule. If I do not punish you, then the rules will mean nothing. We will have chaos in this class. Take off your coat." The boy continued to cry, and a second time he said, "Please don't make me take off my coat." The teacher said, "This is going to hurt me as much as you. Take off your coat and bend over the desk."

Then the boy said, "Sir, I don't mind the punishment, but I only have one shirt, and it's home in the laundry. If I take off my coat everyone will see I do not have a shirt on and they will laugh at me. I don't mind the punishment, but I couldn't bear the embarrassment."

Now there was a dilemma for the teacher. He knew something no one else knew. He wanted to extend mercy. He also knew that every student was watching to see if he would punish the boy. The moments passed on. Then suddenly from the back of the room the bully came forward, took the little boy by the hand, ushered him back to his seat, then came forward, took off his coat, and received the seven lashes for the little boy. (Adapted from "He Took My Whipping for Me," published by the Christian Workers' Tract League, Vancouver, B.C., Canada.)

In chapter 42 of Alma, verse 25, we read: "What, do ye suppose that mercy can rob justice? I say unto you, Nay, not one whit. If so, God would cease to be God." In his great love, the Savior suffered the demands of justice, and thus mercy has been extended through our Redeemer.

Administration to the sick is an ordinance that nearly all Melchizedek Priesthood holders have opportunity to perform. Most find it difficult. I wrestle with the Spirit every time I am asked to administer to the sick. I have confidence in the faith of the individual, confidence and a witness that I have the power of the priesthood, and yet there seems to be a constant worry that my desire to always heal and make better might cause me to not hear the whisperings of the Spirit. Many times blessings are given and we say things that even we question after the blessing.

Many years ago I gave a young mother a blessing. She

had cancer and was going to the hospital for surgery. She had asked if I would give her a blessing, which I did. Before the blessing we talked about her. She had three young children and her husband had left her. She said, "Would you please ask God if I can live long enough to raise my children. I don't mind dying as far as I am concerned, but my children need me." We knelt and had a prayer, exercising every particle of faith all of us had. Then a good brother anointed and I sealed the anointing. Before the operation the doctors did not give her many months to live, and when the operation was over a miracle had happened. It has been many years since the operation, and her children are pretty well grown. I recently learned that she had passed away. The doctors knew far more, technologically speaking, than the elders did, but through the power of the priesthood miracles still happen.

Some years back I ordained a bishop in Texas. During the ordination I told him that he would become very ill, but not to worry, because he would recover. During the blessing I told him that the mantle of bishop, as it were, would transfer to the first counselor during his illness, that the ward would continue to function as though the bishop were there. When I set apart the first counselor in the bishopric, I gave him the other half of the blessing. I told him that during the bishop's illness he would have the mantle transferred to him and that he would be able to direct the ward and preside in a way as though the bishop were there.

On the plane on the way home I thought and thought about the blessings. I questioned whether they were inspiration or an impression. I worried a great deal about them. About two years later I was called to preside over the Texas San Antonio Mission. At a stake conference in Austin I met a bishop. He said, "Do you remember me?" I told him I thought I had probably met him when I visited the Austin Texas Stake conference previously. He said, "That is right, and you ordained me a bishop. Do you remember what you said in the blessing?" I told him that we give many blessings and I was sorry I could not remember. He said, "You told me that I would become very ill, but that I was not to worry, because I would recover, and the mantle during my illness would transfer to my counselor." I said, "I remember. I have worried a great deal about that blessing." He said, "Some months after I had been called to be a bishop I had a heart attack and was laid up for several months. As soon as it happened we thought about the blessing and remembered that you had said not to worry, that I would get well. The mantle transferred to the first counselor, and the ward hardly missed a stride during the five months I was recuperating." There is power in the priesthood. The sick can be healed and miracles can happen.

One of the sad notes of blessings is the person who desires a blessing because nothing else has worked and he is desperate. Many times such a person has little faith and considers that "it will not do any harm." The blessing may be given by a worthy priesthood holder, but due to lack of faith or sins in the life of the unrepentant one, there is no healing. Section 58 of the Doctrine and Covenants states:

"Who am I, saith the Lord, that have promised and have not fulfilled? I command and men obey not; I revoke and they receive not the blessing. Then they say in their hearts: This is not the work of the Lord, for his promises are not fulfilled. But wo unto such, for their reward lurketh beneath, and not from above." (D&C 58:31-33.)

Blessings are predicated upon our faithfulness and our faith. I met a good brother on a plane from California. He said to me, "You were at our stake a few years back, and you told a story about a young man whose father blessed him after he had been electrocuted and his life had been spared." He continued, "I went hunting with my son. I sent him over to one ridge and I headed another direction with the idea of working up toward him. Suddenly I had an impression to get to him as fast as I could." When he finally arrived where the boy should have been, he saw him lying at the bottom of a steep cliff. I believe he said that the boy had fallen and rolled at least sixty-five feet. He made his way down to his son and examined him. The youth appeared to be all broken up, his head bloody and covered with lacerations. The father continued, "I remembered the story you told. I laid my hands upon his head and, by the power of the priesthood and in the name of the Lord Jesus Christ, I promised him he would live." It was some time before the paramedics arrived, and as they rode to the hospital the paramedic in the back with the boy said, "Did you give him a blessing?" The father said he had. The paramedic said, "I guess that is all that can be done for him." This brother told me that today there is hardly a scar on the young man. He is healthy and strong. Faith does precede the miracle.

Generally, when there is time, I always put on my suit, shirt, and tie before administering to the sick. Some time ago I got up one morning and was getting ready to go to work. While I was shaving, I noticed my wife had written on the mirror, "Honey, when you are up and dressed, would you give me a special blessing? I have a problem." When I had my suit and tie on, I went to give her a blessing. After the blessing I said, "How long have you had the problem?" She said, "Since about two o'clock." I said, "Why didn't you awaken me?" She said, "I knew you would get up and get dressed, put on your white shirt, tie, and suit. I guess no one else knows how much you need your sleep and how tired you are except me, and I couldn't do that to you." I said, "Merlene, what would I do if anyone else in the Church wanted a blessing?" She said, "You would dress appropriately no matter what the hour." I said, "That's right, and don't you think I would rather do it for you than anyone else in the whole world? Don't deprive me of giving you a blessing when you need one."

We read in the Doctrine and Covenants: "And again, it shall come to pass that he that hath faith in me to be healed, and is not appointed unto death, shall be healed." (D&C 42:48.)

Ordinances in the temple are sacred and cannot be discussed outside the temple walls. These ordinances are reserved for the "elect" and are predicated also upon our faithfulness. Celestial marriage for time and all eternity is one of the ordinances of the temple. This ordinance must be sealed by the Holy Spirit of Promise. Thus no man or woman can deceive or lie his or her way through this ordinance and have it valid. "The more sure word of prophecy means a man's knowing that he is sealed up unto eternal life, by revelation and the spirit of prophecy, through the power of the Holy Priesthood." (D&C 131:5.)

Few men on this earth have been given the sealing powers. As a General Authority, I have been blessed with the sealing powers. It has been my privilege to seal many young couples at the altars of the temples. There are some who come unworthily to have a marriage performed in the temple. The sealing does not take place at that time because of unworthiness. Later in life, if repentance is complete and sincere, the sealing is validated by the Holy Spirit of Promise. In some cases that never takes place, and couples may wake up in eternity to find out that their lives have never qualified them for the sealing. In other cases I have been privileged to perform sealings where I knew by the Spirit that a temple marriage was literally a celestial sealing, sealed by the Holy Spirit of Promise.

The subject of ordinances is so broad, it could fill several volumes. In these few pages I have tried to share with you the sacred nature of all ordinances. They must not be taken lightly, but must be performed by authorized agents who have the authority. Each of us should endeavor, with all our souls, to keep every covenant we make through these ordinances. To be exalted, a person must be baptized and confirmed in the Church of Jesus Christ. Every soul must receive his or her endowment. Every male must receive the Melchizedek Priesthood, and a man and a woman must be sealed in the new and everlasting covenant of temple marriage. All must live worthily, keep the commandments, serve their fellowmen, and endure to the end. These blessings are available to all who qualify through worthiness. No righteous member of the Church will be denied any of the ordinances that exalt as long as he or she shall continue to the end in worthiness. The ordinances may take place in this life or in the life to come, but they will take place.

HEALING: A SPECIAL PRIESTHOOD BLESSING

Elder L. Tom Perry

One of the significant indications that the Lord has established his work and is directing his children on earth is the priesthood. This blessing was bestowed on mankind to enable man to act in the Lord's name in all things as the Lord directs.

As the Savior began his earthly ministry, he called "unto him twelve disciples," and gave them power to assist him in his earthly responsibilities.

"He gave them power against unclean spirits, to cast them out, and to heal all manner of sickness and all manner of disease. . . .

"These twelve Jesus sent forth, and commanded them, saying, Go not into the way of the Gentiles, and into any city of the Samaritans enter ye not: But go rather to the lost sheep of the house of Israel.

"And as ye go, preach, saying, The kingdom of heaven is at hand. Heal the sick, cleanse the lepers, raise the dead, cast out devils: freely ye have received, freely give." (Matthew 10:1, 5-8.)

The Book of Mormon bears a second witness of this power being given to mankind. The account is told of Nephi, one of the Nephite disciples, administering to the needs of the people:

"And it came to pass that Nephi—having been visited by angels and also the voice of the Lord, therefore having seen angels, and being eye-witness, and having had power given unto him that he might know concerning the ministry of Christ, and also being eye-witness to their quick return from righteousness unto their wickedness and abominations;

"Therefore, being grieved for the hardness of their hearts and the blindness of their minds—went forth among them in that same year, and began to testify, boldly, repentance and remission of sins through faith on the Lord Jesus Christ.

"And he did minister many things unto them; and all of them cannot be written, and a part of them would not suffice, therefore they are not written in this book. And Nephi did minister with power and with great authority. . . .

"And as many as had devils cast out from them, and were healed of their sicknesses and their infirmities, did truly manifest unto the people that they had been wrought upon by the Spirit of God, and had been healed; and they did show forth signs also and did do some miracles among the people." (3 Nephi 7:15-17, 22.)

Numerous accounts of healing by the power of the holy priesthood are recorded in the history of the Church. One that has always impressed me the most occurred at the time of the founding of Nauvoo.

It was a most difficult time for the Saints. They had been forced from their homes in Missouri in the dead of winter, and their hope of establishing a new Zion had all but faded. The Prophet Joseph Smith had spent long months in jail at Liberty, Missouri, on false charges, and was awaiting trial. Thus the Saints had to leave the state without his inspired leadership.

During the late winter and early spring months the Saints tried to provide shelter for their families. What a sad sight it must have been for the Prophet, when he finally gained his freedom, to find them enduring such hardships, living in tents, caves, and whatever housing could be found.

Despite these hardships, however, there seemed to be no question in the minds of the Saints that they would find another place of gathering. Residents of communities along the Mississippi River in Illinois and Iowa were friendly toward them. The call was once again sounded to gather, this time to a place that would be called Nauvoo, on the Illinois side of the Mississippi. Then the process of building started once again.

Weakened by the ordeal of the expulsion from Missouri, the people were susceptible to much illness. The Prophet gave up his home to shelter many of those who were ill, and he was living in a tent when he found himself ill with fever. Miraculously, one morning he seemed strong and well. As he looked out at the suffering of his people, he called upon the power of God and went among the sick on both sides of the river. Many miraculous healings resulted from the power he exercised that day. The manifestation of the priesthood gave the Saints new hope, and they were again able to turn their energies toward building a new center for the Church.

The healing power of the priesthood has always been manifest to the children of our Father in heaven according to their faith. We witnessed another great miracle of healing during a recent general conference.

The Brethren had been concerned about the health of President Spencer W. Kimball. His voice was weak, and it was evident in our associations with him that he was not well. We met in the Salt Lake Temple for our usual fast and testimony meeting before general conference, and President Kimball called on Elder Mark E. Petersen to bear his testimony first. In his testimony Elder Petersen asked the Brethren to exercise more faith in behalf of President Kimball. He talked about the healing power of the priesthood, and asked us to exercise it for our prophet so that he would be blessed through the conference and beyond in the difficult schedule ahead of him.

The Brethren exercised their priesthood, and blessings were manifest in President Kimball's behalf. A miracle occurred! He was stronger the next day and continued to become stronger each day thereafter. We were privileged to see, to hear, and to enjoy his great discourse on love as he concluded the general conference. The miracle did not stop at the conclusion of the conference, however. He seemed to be renewed in strength each day as he traveled to Asia to hold many area conferences and to dedicate the Tokyo Temple. He returned home after this successful trip of blessing the Saints, only to go into a week filled with activities and meetings and the dedication of another temple, in Seattle, Washington.

I have always been grateful that I was reared in a home where parents understood the power and use of the priesthood. This knowledge was transmitted from parents to children by the bearing of testimony and by the exercise of that power.

My father was serving as our bishop at the time I received the Melchizedek Priesthood. He wanted to be certain I understood the blessing of it. Not long after my ordination, I was invited to function with him in consecrating a bottle of oil for use in the healing of the sick. As opportunities arose in our ward, he invited me to accompany him to visit the sick, and to anoint with the consecrated oil those in need.

About the time I was ready to leave on my mission, Dad was taken to the hospital for an operation. He requested a blessing at the hands of the elders, and I was asked to accompany Elder ElRay L. Christiansen, who was later called to be an Assistant to the Council of the Twelve, to give a blessing to my father. As we entered the hospital room, I prepared to anoint him. Dad took this occasion to teach me yet another lesson. He turned to Elder Christiansen and said, "Will you please anoint." Then he turned to me and asked if I would seal the anointing. I remember how kind Elder Christiansen was in complying with the request of my father, and how this further taught me about the healing power of the priesthood as we performed that sacred ordinance together.

I am grateful for the power of the priesthood. My experience has shown me that its power increases with the faith we exercise in it. I am thankful for the privilege of bearing the Melchizedek Priesthood. What a comfort it has been in my life! I witnessed the blessings of its power as a young elder in the mission field and as a United States Marine on the battlefield, and I have witnessed its blessings as a father in the home and as an ecclesiastical leader in my various Church responsibilities. I bear you my personal witness of that healing power, a special priesthood blessing.

POWER IN
THE PRIESTHOOD

Elder J. Thomas Fyans

Wherever we look, we see evidence of man's creative genius and his utilization of power. We see great movements of people in giant airplanes flying through space with a speed approaching and, in some cases, beyond that of sound.

We see spacecraft launched and, by a signal sent from earth, breaking the drag of gravity and going into space to orbit our planet as explorers of the universe, traveling thousands of miles per hour.

We see nuclear power harnessed to warm us in winter, to cool us in summer, to chill and preserve our food, to bake or broil it upon command.

We hear the roar of motors in great factories as power is furnished for industry.

Great turbines, whirling under the crush of water, vibrate and send light to cities and homes.

How magnificent is the power of man!

Is there any way that the power of the priesthood can be measured against this display of man's tremendous might?

Let us begin the quest for understanding God's power by peering into the stable and seeing a babe wrapped in swaddling clothes lying in a manger.

"And so it was, that, while they were there, the days were accomplished that she should be delivered. And she brought forth her firstborn son, and wrapped him in swaddling clothes, and laid him in a manger; because there was no room for them in the inn." (Luke 2:6-7.)

The heavens open, and a witness bears testimony:

"And the angel said unto them, Fear not: for, behold, I bring you good tidings of great joy, which shall be to all people. For unto you is born this day in the city of David a Saviour, which is Christ the Lord." (Luke 2:10-11.)

We next see him being presented in the temple:

"And when the days of her purification according to the law of Moses were accomplished, they brought him to Jerusalem, to present him to the Lord." (Luke 2:22.)

In the temple, Simeon, a just and devout man under the influence of the Holy Ghost, shares this revelation: "And it was revealed unto him by the Holy Ghost, that he should not see death, before he had seen the Lord's Christ." (Luke 2:26.) Simeon bears witness that he has seen the Redeemer.

Time has passed; the child is now a young man.

"Now his parents went to Jerusalem every year at the feast of the passover. And when he was twelve years old, they went up to Jerusalem after the custom of the feast. And when they had fulfilled the days, as they returned, the child Jesus tarried behind in Jerusalem; and Joseph and his mother knew not of it.

"But they, supposing him to have been in the company, went a day's journey; and they sought him among their kinsfolk and acquaintance. And when they found him not, they turned back again to Jerusalem, seeking him.

"And it came to pass, that after three days they found him in the temple, sitting in the midst of the doctors, both hearing them, and asking them questions. And all that heard him were astonished at his understanding and answers.

"And when they saw him, they were amazed; and his mother said unto him, Son, why hast thou thus dealt with us? behold, thy father and I have sought thee sorrowing.

"And he said unto them, How is it that ye sought me? wist ye not that I must be about my Father's business?

"And they understood not the saying which he spake unto them." (Luke 2:41-50.)

The Savior is baptized by John, setting for us a pattern of obedience to important teachings:

"Now when all the people were baptized, it came to pass, that Jesus also being baptized, and praying, the heaven was opened. And the Holy Ghost descended in a bodily shape like a dove upon him, and a voice came from heaven, which said, Thou art my beloved Son; in thee I am well pleased. And Jesus himself began to be about thirty years of age, being (as was supposed) the son of Joseph, which was the son of Heli." (Luke 3:21-23.)

The power to resist temptation is demonstrated:

"Then was Jesus led up of the Spirit into the wilderness to be tempted of the devil. And when he had fasted forty days and forty nights, he was afterward an hungred.

"And when the tempter came to him, he said, If thou be the Son of God, command that these stones be made bread.

"But he answered and said, It is written, Man shall not live by bread alone, but by every word that proceedeth out of the mouth of God.

"Then the devil taketh him up into the holy city, and setteth him on a pinnacle of the temple, And saith unto him, If thou be the Son of God, cast thyself down: for it is written, He shall give his angels charge concerning thee: and in their hands they shall bear thee up, lest at any time thou dash thy foot against a stone.

"Jesus said unto him, It is written again, Thou shalt not tempt the Lord thy God.

"Again, the devil taketh him up into an exceeding high mountain, and sheweth him all the kingdoms of the world, and the glory of them; And saith unto him, All these things will I give thee, if thou wilt fall down and worship me.

"Then saith Jesus unto him, Get thee hence, Satan: for it is written, Thou shalt worship the Lord thy God, and him only shalt thou serve.

"Then the devil leaveth him, and, behold, angels came and ministered unto him." (Matthew 4:1-11.)

Power over the elements is manifest as he stills the storm:

"Now it came to pass on a certain day, that he went into a ship with his disciples: and he said unto them, Let us go over unto the other side of the lake. And they launched forth.

"But as they sailed he fell asleep: and there came down a storm of wind on the lake; and they were filled with water, and were in jeopardy.

"And they came to him, and awoke him, saying, Master,

master, we perish. Then he arose, and rebuked the wind and the raging of the water: and they ceased, and there was a calm.

"And he said unto them, Where is your faith? And they being afraid wondered, saying one to another, What manner of man is this! for he commandeth even the winds and water, and they obey him." (Luke 8:22-25.)

The miraculous feeding of the five thousand is but a hint of the real power of the Redeemer.

"When Jesus then lifted up his eyes, and saw a great company come unto him, he saith unto Philip, Whence shall we buy bread, that these may eat?

"One of his disciples, Andrew, Simon Peter's brother, saith unto him, There is a lad here, which hath five barley loaves, and two small fishes: but what are they among so many?

"And Jesus said, Make the men sit down. Now there was much grass in the place. So the men sat down, in number about five thousand. And Jesus took the loaves; and when he had given thanks, he distributed to the disciples, and the disciples to them that were set down; and likewise of the fishes as much as they would.

"When they were filled, he said unto his disciples, Gather up the fragments that remain, that nothing be lost.

"Therefore they gathered them together, and filled twelve baskets with the fragments of the five barley loaves, which remained over and above unto them that had eaten.

"Then those men, when they had seen the miracle that Jesus did, said, This is of a truth that prophet that should come into the world." (John 6:5, 8-14.)

His healing power gives sight to the blind:

"And he cometh to Bethsaida; and they bring a blind man unto him, and besought him to touch him.

"And he took the blind man by the hand, and led him out of the town; and when he had spit on his eyes, and put his hands upon him, he asked him if he saw ought.

"And he looked up, and said, I see men as trees, walking.

"After that he put his hands again upon his eyes, and

made him look up: and he was restored, and saw every man clearly.

"And he sent him away to his house, saying, Neither go into the town, nor tell it to any in the town." (Mark 8:22-26.)

He restores life to him who is dead:

"Then when Jesus came, he found that he had lain in the grave four days already.

"Then said Martha unto Jesus, Lord, if thou hadst been here, my brother had not died.

"And [Jesus] said, Where have ye laid him: They said unto him, Lord, come and see.

"Then they took away the stone from the place where the dead was laid. And Jesus lifted up his eyes, and said, Father, I thank thee that thou hast heard me.

"And when he thus had spoken, he cried with a loud voice, Lazarus, come forth. And he that was dead came forth." (John 11:17, 21, 34, 41, 43-44.)

Lazarus's blessing of continued mortal life is subsequently surpassed by the movement into eternal realms of One who had lived here on this earth:

"In the end of the sabbath, as it began to dawn toward the first day of the week, came Mary Magdalene and the other Mary to see the sepulchre.

"And the angel answered and said unto the women, Fear not ye: for I know that ye seek Jesus, which was crucified. He is not here: for he is risen, as he said. Come, see the place where the Lord lay. And go quickly, and tell his disciples that he is risen from the dead; and, behold, he goeth before you into Galilee; there shall ye see him: lo, I have told you.

"And they departed quickly from the sepulchre with fear and great joy; and did run to bring his disciples word. And as they went to tell his disciples, behold, Jesus met them, saying, All hail. And they came and held him by the feet, and worshipped him." (Matthew 28:1,5-9.)

The pattern is established; the bands of death are broken; the resurrection actually occurs!

He appears to his disciples to further instruct them:

"And after eight days again his disciples were within, and Thomas with them: then came Jesus, the doors being shut, and stood in the midst, and said, Peace be unto you." (John 20:26.)

Having completed his earthly mission in the Holy Land, he bids farewell to his trusted followers:

"And he led them out as far as to Bethany, and he lifted up his hands, and blessed them. And it came to pass, while he blessed them, he was parted from them, and carried up into heaven." (Luke 24:50-51.)

Heavenly powers are imparted to his disciples.

In the Prophet Joseph Smith's inspired translation of Genesis, we catch a glimpse of the force given through ordination to the Melchizedek Priesthood:

"And Melchizedek lifted up his voice and blessed Abram. . . . It being after the order of the Son of God; . . .

"For God having sworn unto Enoch and unto his seed with an oath by himself; that every one being ordained after this order and calling should have power, by faith, to break mountains, to divide the seas, to dry up waters, to turn them out of their course;

"To put at defiance the armies of nations, to divide the earth, to break every band, to stand in the presence of God; to do all things according to his will, according to his command, subdue principalities and powers; and this by the will of the Son of God which was from before the foundation of the world." (Genesis 14:25, 28, 30-31.)

We learn of the eternal nature and authority of the Melchizedek Priesthood by listening as the Prophet Joseph Smith preaches a sermon in a conference in October 1840:

"Its institution was prior to 'the foundation of this earth, or the morning stars sang together, or the Sons of God shouted for joy,' and is the highest and holiest Priesthood, and is after the order of the Son of God, and all other Priesthoods are only parts, ramifications, powers and blessings belonging to the same, and are held, controlled, and directed by it. It is the channel through which the Almighty commenced revealing His glory at the beginning of the creation of this earth, and through which He has continued to reveal Himself to the children of men to the present time, and through which He will make known His purposes to the end of time." (*Teachings of the Prophet Joseph Smith*, Deseret Book, 1976, p. 167.)

Recognizing this power as eternal, does it transcend this sphere on which we live? Joseph Fielding Smith, Jr., a son of President Joseph Fielding Smith, clarifies this:

"Priesthood is the power of God. It is everlasting because God is everlasting. By this power the heavens exist and worlds without number have been created, are being created, and will be created. Through priesthood, all things move in their times and their seasons. Without it, nothing would exist. Priesthood is authority delegated to man by which he is permitted to officiate in the ordinances of the gospel as an official representative of God." (*Religious Truths Defined*, Bookcraft, 1959, pp. 235-36.)

May we be enlightened by the Spirit of truth to comprehend these great creative forces of the priesthood. In the first chapter of Genesis, our depth of understanding is immeasurably increased:

"In the beginning God created the heaven and the earth.

"So God created man in his own image, in the image of God created he him; male and female created he them. And God blessed them, and God said unto them, Be fruitful and multiply, and replenish the earth, and subdue it." (Genesis 1:1, 27-28.)

In the New Testament we find these truths:

"For by him were all things created, that are in heaven, and that are in earth, visible and invisible, whether they be thrones, or dominions, or principalities, or powers: all things were created by him, and for him: And he is before all things, and by him all things consist." (Colossians 1:16-17.)

The Book of Mormon adds its witness:

"And now, my sons, I speak unto you these things for your profit and learning; for there is a God, and he hath created all things, both the heavens and the earth, and all things that in them are, both things to act and things to be acted upon." (2 Nephi 2:14.)

"And he shall be called Jesus Christ, the Son of God, the

Father of heaven and earth, the Creator of all things from the beginning." (Mosiah 3:8.)

Testimony in the revelations of the fulness of times contributes this understanding:

"For we saw him, even on the right hand of God; and we heard the voice bearing record that he is the Only Begotten of the Father—That by him, and through him, and of him, the worlds are and were created, and the inhabitants thereof are begotten sons and daughters unto God." (D&C 76:23-24.)

We are lifted to lofty peaks in this great sweeping summary of the power of the priesthood:

"This is the light of Christ. As also he is in the sun, and the light of the sun, and the power thereof by which it was made.

"As also he is in the moon, and is the light of the moon, and the power thereof by which it was made; As also the light of the stars, and the power thereof by which they were made; And the earth also, and the power thereof, even the earth upon which you stand.

"And the light which shineth, which giveth you light, is through him who enlighteneth your eyes, which is the same light that quickeneth your understandings; Which light proceedeth forth from the presence of God to fill the immensity of space—The light which is in all things, which giveth life to all things, which is the law by which all things are governed, even the power of God who sitteth upon his throne, who is in the bosom of eternity, who is in the midst of all things.

"Now, verily I say unto you, that through the redemption which is made for you is brought to pass the resurrection from the dead. And the spirit and the body are the soul of man." (D&C 88:7-15.)

We must not be earthbound in our comprehension of these magnificent powers. Let us soar into the heavens where our heights of perception will be quickened.

"And worlds without number have I created; and I also created them for mine own purpose." (Moses 1:33.)

"And as one earth shall pass away, and the heavens thereof even so shall another come; and there is no end to my works, neither to my words." (Moses 1:38.)

"And were it possible that man could number the particles of the earth, yea, millions of earths like this, it would not be a beginning to the number of thy creations; and thy curtains are stretched out still; and yet thou art there, and thy bosom is there; and also thou art just; thou art merciful and kind forever." (Moses 7:30.)

What is the power of ordinary man?

To discover what already exists—what the Lord already knows. To use the tiniest particles of the creation to fly airplanes, put spacecraft into orbit, light cities and homes. The relative size of a manmade satellite compared to the magnificent creations of the universe gives us some inkling of the comparison of earthbound powers to those priesthood powers that distill upon us from the heavens.

What is the power of the priesthood?

To bless a tiny infant cradled in our arms. To bless the sick and the lame. To seal on earth that it might be sealed in the heavens. To administer other sacred ordinances. Or to create an earth or a universe.

"Verily, verily, I say unto you, He that believeth on me, the works that I do shall he do also; and greater works than these shall he do." (John 14:12.)

THE NEW
REVELATION
ON PRIESTHOOD

Elder Bruce R. McConkie

I was present when the Lord revealed to President Spencer W. Kimball that the time had come, in His eternal providences, to offer the fulness of the gospel and the blessings of the holy priesthood to all men.

I was present, with my brethren of the Twelve and the counselors in the First Presidency, when all of us heard the same voice and received the same message from on high.

It was on a glorious June day in 1978. All of us were together in an upper room in the Salt Lake Temple. We were engaged in fervent prayer, pleading with the Lord to manifest his mind and will concerning those who are entitled to receive his holy priesthood. President Kimball himself was mouth, offering the desires of his heart and of our hearts to that God whose servants we are.

In his prayer President Kimball asked that all of us might be cleansed and made free from sin so that we might receive the Lord's word. He counseled freely and fully with the Lord, was given utterance by the power of the Spirit, and what he said was inspired from on high. It was one of those rare and seldom-experienced times when the disciples of the Lord are perfectly united, when every heart beats as one, and when the same Spirit burns in every bosom.

I have thought since that our united prayer must have been like that of the Nephite disciples—the Lord's Twelve in that day and for that people—who "were gathered together and were united in mighty prayer and fasting" to learn the name that the Lord had given to his church. (See 3 Nephi 27:1-3.) In their day the Lord came personally to answer their petition; in our day he sent his Spirit to deliver the message.

And as it was with our Nephite brethren of old, so it was with us. We too had come together in the spirit of true worship and with unity of desire. We were all fasting and had just concluded a meeting of some three hours' duration that was attended by nearly all of the General Authorities. That meeting also was held in the room of the First Presidency and the Twelve in the holy temple. In it we had been counseled by the First Presidency, had heard the messages and testimonies of about fifteen of the brethren, had renewed our covenants, in the ordinance of the sacrament, to serve God and keep his commandments that we might always have his Spirit to be with us, and, surrounding the holy altar, had offered up the desires of our hearts to the Lord. After this meeting, which was one of great spiritual uplift and enlightenment, all of the brethren except those in the Presidency and the Twelve were excused.

When we were alone by ourselves in that sacred place where we meet weekly to wait upon the Lord, to seek guidance from his Spirit, and to transact the affairs of his earthly kingdom, President Kimball brought up the matter of the possible conferral of the priesthood upon those of all races. This was a subject that the group of us had discussed at length on numerous occasions in the preceding weeks and months. The President restated the problem involved, reminded us of our prior discussions, and said he had spent many days alone in this upper room pleading with the Lord for an answer to our prayers. He said that if the answer was to continue our present course of denying the priesthood to the seed of Cain, as the Lord had theretofore directed, he was prepared to defend that decision to the death. But, he said, if the long-sought day had come in which the curse of the past was to be removed, he thought we might prevail upon the Lord so to indicate. He expressed the hope that we might receive a clear answer one way or the other so the matter might be laid to rest.

At this point President Kimball asked the brethren if any of them desired to express their feelings and views as to the matter in hand. We all did so, freely and fluently and at considerable length, each person stating his views and manifesting the feelings of his heart. There was a marvelous outpouring of unity, oneness, and agreement in the council. This session continued for somewhat more than two hours. Then President Kimball suggested that we unite in formal prayer and said, modestly, that if it was agreeable with the rest of us he would act as voice.

It was during this prayer that the revelation came. The Spirit of the Lord rested mightily upon us all; we felt something akin to what happened on the day of Pentecost and at the dedication of the Kirtland Temple. From the midst of eternity, the voice of God, conveyed by the power of the Spirit, spoke to his prophet. The message was that the time had now come to offer the fulness of the everlasting gospel, including celestial marriage, and the priesthood, and the blessings of the temple, to all men, without reference to race or color, solely on the basis of personal worthiness. And we all heard the same voice, received the same message, and became personal witnesses that the word received was the mind and will and voice of the Lord.

President Kimball's prayer was answered and our prayers were answered. He heard the voice and we heard the same voice. All doubt and uncertainty fled. He knew the answer and we knew the answer. And we are all living witnesses of the truthfulness of the word so graciously sent from heaven.

The ancient curse is no more. The seed of Cain and Ham and Canaan and Egyptus and Pharaoh—all these now have power to rise up and bless Abraham as their father. All these, gentile in lineage, may now come and inherit by adoption all the blessings of Abraham, Isaac, and Jacob. All these may now be numbered with those in the one fold of the one Shepherd who is Lord of all.

In the days that followed the receipt of the new revelation, President Kimball and President Ezra Taft Benson—the senior and most spiritually experienced ones among us—both said, expressing the feelings of us all, that neither of them had ever experienced anything of such spiritual magnitude and power as was poured out upon the Presidency and the Twelve that day in the upper room in the house of the Lord. And of it I say: It is true; I was there; I heard the voice; and the Lord be praised that it has come to pass in our day.

Not long after this revelation came, I was scheduled to address nearly a thousand seminary and institute teachers on a Book of Mormon subject. After I arrived on the stand, Brother Joe J. Christensen, under whose direction the symposium was going forward, asked me to depart from my prepared talk and give those assembed some guidance relative to the new revelation. He asked if I would take 2 Nephi 26:33 as a text. This I agreed to do, and, accordingly, spoke the following words:

I would like to say something about the new revelation relative to our taking the priesthood to those of all nations and races. "He [meaning Christ, who is the Lord God] inviteth them all to come unto him and partake of his goodness; and he denieth none that come unto him, black and white, bond and free, male and female; and he remembereth the heathen; and all are alike unto God, both Jew and Gentile." (2 Nephi 26:33.)

These words have now taken on a new meaning. We have caught a new vision of their true significance. This also applies to a great number of other passages in the revelations. Since the Lord gave this revelation on the priesthood, our understanding of many passages has expanded. Many of us never imagined or supposed that they had the extensive and broad meaning that they do have.

I shall give you a few impressions relative to what has happened, and then attempt—if properly guided by the Spirit—to indicate to you the great significance that this event has in the Church, in the world, and where the rolling forth of the great gospel is concerned.

The gospel goes to various peoples and nations on a priority basis. We were commanded in the early days of this dispensation to preach the gospel to every nation, kindred, tongue, and people. Our revelations talk about its going to every creature. There was, of course, no possible way for us to do all of this in the beginning days of our dispensation, nor can we now, in the full sense.

And so, guided by inspiration, we began to go from one nation and one culture to another. Some day, in the providences of the Lord, we shall get into Red China and Russia and the Middle East, and so on, until eventually the gospel will have been preached everywhere, to all people; and this will occur before the second coming of the Son of Man.

Not only is the gospel to go, on a priority basis and harmonious to a divine timetable, to one nation after another, but the whole history of God's dealings with men on earth indicates that such has been the case in the past; it has been restricted and limited where many people are concerned. For instance, in the day between Moses and Christ, the gospel went to the house of Israel, almost exclusively. By the time of Jesus, the legal administrators and prophetic associates that he had were so fully indoctrinated with the concept of having the gospel go only to the house of Israel that they were totally unable to envision the true significance of his proclamation that after the resurrection they should then go to all the world. They did not go to the gentile nations initially. In his own ministration, Jesus preached only to the lost sheep of the house of Israel, and had so commanded the apostles. (Matthew 10:6.)

It is true that he made a few minor exceptions because of the faith and devotion of some gentile people. There was one woman who wanted to eat the crumbs that fell from the table of the children, causing him to say, "O woman, great is thy faith." (Matthew 15:28; see also Mark 7:27-28.) With some minor exceptions, the gospel in that day went exclusively to Israel. The Lord had to give Peter the vision and revelation of the sheet coming down from heaven with the unclean meat on it, following which Cornelius sent the messenger to Peter to learn what he, Cornelius, and his gentile associates should do. The Lord commanded them that the gospel should go to the gentiles, and so it was. There was about a quarter of a century, then, in New Testament times, when there were extreme difficulties among the Saints. They were weighing and evaluating, struggling with the problems of whether the gospel was to go only to the house of Israel or whether it now went to all men. Could all men come to him on an equal basis with the seed of Abraham?

There have been these problems, and the Lord has permitted them to arise. There isn't any question about that.

We do not envision the whole reason and purpose behind all of it; we can only suppose and reason that it is on the basis of preexistence and of our premortal devotion and faith.

You know this principle: God "hath made of one blood all nations of men for to dwell on all the face of the earth, and hath determined the times before appointed, and the bounds of their habitation; That they should seek the Lord, if haply they might feel after him, and find him" (Acts 17:26-27)—meaning that there is an appointed time for successive nations and peoples and races and cultures to be offered the saving truths of the gospel. There are nations today to whom we have not gone—notably Red China and Russia. But you can rest assured that we will fulfill the requirement of taking the gospel to those nations before the second coming of the Son of Man.

And I have no hesitancy whatever in saying that before the Lord comes, in all those nations we will have congregations that are stable, secure, devoted, and sound. We will have stakes of Zion. We will have people who have progressed in spiritual things to the point where they have received all of the blessings of the house of the Lord. That is the destiny.

We have revelations that tell us that the gospel is to go to every nation, kindred, tongue, and people before the second coming of the Son of Man. And we have revelations that recite that when the Lord comes, he will find those who speak every tongue and are members of every nation and kindred, who will be kings and priests, who will live and reign on earth with him a thousand years. That means, as you know, that people from all nations will have the blessings of the house of the Lord before the Second Coming.

We have read these passages and their associated passages for many years. We have seen what the words say and have said to ourselves, "Yes, it says that, but we must read out of it the taking of the gospel and the blessings of the temple to the Negro people, because they are denied certain things." There are statements in our literature by the early brethren that we have interpreted to mean that the Negroes would not receive the priesthood in mortality. I have said the same things, and people write me letters and say, "You said such and such, and how is it now that we do such and such?" And all I can say to that is that it is time disbelieving people repented and got in line and believed in a living, modern prophet. Forget everything that I have said, or what President Brigham Young or President George Q. Cannon or whosoever has said in days past that is contrary to the present revelation. We spoke with a limited understanding and without the light and knowledge that now has come into the world.

We get our truth and our light line upon line and precept upon precept. We have now had added a new flood of intelligence and light on this particular subject, and it erases all the darkness and all the views and all the thoughts of the past. They don't matter any more.

It doesn't make a particle of difference what anybody ever said about the Negro matter before the first day of June 1978. It is a new day and a new arrangement, and the Lord has now given the revelation that sheds light out into the world on this subject. As to any slivers of light or any particles of darkness of the past, we forget about them. We now do what meridian Israel did when the Lord said the gospel should go to the gentiles. We forget all the statements that limited the gospel to the house of Israel, and we start going to the gentiles.

Obviously, the Brethren have had a great anxiety and concern about this problem for a long period of time, and President Spencer W. Kimball has been exercised and has sought the Lord in faith. When we seek the Lord on a matter, with sufficient faith and devotion, he gives us an answer. You will recall that the Book of Mormon teaches that if the apostles in Jerusalem had asked the Lord, he would have told them about the Nephites. But they didn't ask, and they didn't manifest the faith—and they didn't get an answer. One underlying reason for what happened to us is that the Brethren asked in faith; they petitioned and desired and wanted an answer—President Kimball in particular. And the other underlying principle is that in the eternal providences of the Lord, the time had come for extending the gospel to a race and a culture to whom it had previously been denied, at least as far as all of its blessings are concerned. So it was a matter of faith and righteousness and seeking on the one hand, and it was a matter of the divine timetable on the other hand. The time had arrived when the gospel, with all its blessings and obligations, should go to the Negro.

Well, in that setting, on the first day of June 1978, the First Presidency and the Twelve, after full discussion of the proposition and all the premises and principles that are involved, importuned the Lord for a revelation. President Kimball was mouth, and he prayed with great faith and great fervor; this was one of those occasions when an inspired prayer was offered. You know the Doctrine and Covenants statement, that if we pray by the power of the Spirit we will receive answers to our prayers and it will be given us what we shall ask. (D&C 50:30.) It was given President Kimball what he should ask. He prayed by the power of the Spirit, and there was perfect unity, total and complete harmony, between the Presidency and the Twelve on the issue involved.

And when President Kimball finished his prayer, the Lord gave a revelation by the power of the Holy Ghost. Revelation primarily comes by the power of the Holy Ghost. Always that member of the Godhead is involved. But most revelations, from the beginning to now, have come in that way. There have been revelations given in various ways on other occasions. The Father and the Son appeared in the Sacred Grove. Moroni, an angel from heaven, came relative to the Book of Mormon and the plates and relative to instructing the Prophet in the affairs that were destined to occur in this dispensation. There have been visions, notably the vision of the degrees of glory. There may be an infinite number of ways that God can ordain that revelations come. But, primarily, revelation comes by the power of the Holy Ghost. The principle is set forth in the Doctrine and Covenants, section 68, that whatever the elders of the Church speak, when moved upon by the power of the Holy Ghost, shall be scripture, shall be the mind and will and voice of the Lord.

On this occasion, because of the importuning and the faith, and because the hour and the time had arrived, the

Lord in his providences poured out the Holy Ghost upon the First Presidency and the Twelve in a miraculous and marvelous manner, beyond anything that any then present had ever experienced. The revelation came to the President of the Church; it also came to each individual present. There were ten members of the Council of the Twelve and three of the First Presidency there assembled. The result was that President Kimball knew, and each one of us knew, independent of any other person, by direct and personal revelation to us, that the time had now come to extend the gospel and all its blessings and all its obligations, including the priesthood and the blessings of the house of the Lord, to those of every nation, culture, and race, including the black race. There was no question whatsoever as to what happened or as to the word and message that came.

The revelation came to the President of the Church and, in harmony with Church government, was announced by him; the announcement was made eight days later over the signature of the First Presidency. But in this instance, in addition to the revelation coming to the man who would announce it to the Church and to the world, and who was sustained as the mouthpiece of God on earth, the revelation came to every member of the body that I have named. They all knew it in the temple.

In my judgment this was done by the Lord in this way because it was a revelation of such tremendous significance and import; one that would reverse the whole direction of the Church, procedurally and administratively; one that would affect the living and the dead; one that would affect the total relationship that we have with the world; one, I say, of such significance that the Lord wanted independent witnesses who could bear record that the thing had happened.

Now if President Kimball had received the revelation and had asked for a sustaining vote, obviously he would have received it and the revelation would have been announced. But the Lord chose this other course, in my judgment, because of the tremendous import and the eternal significance of what was being revealed. This affects our missionary work and all of our preaching to the world. This affects our genealogical research and all of our temple ordinances. This affects what is going on in the spirit world, because the gospel is preached in the spirit world preparatory to men's receiving the vicarious ordinances that make them heirs to salvation and exaltation. This is a revelation of tremendous significance.

The vision of the degrees of glory begins by saying, "Hear, O ye heavens, and give ear, O earth." (D&C 76:1.) In other words, in that revelation the Lord was announcing truth to heaven and to earth because those principles of salvation operate on both sides of the veil; and salvation is administered to an extent here to men, and it is administered to another extent in the spirit world. We correlate and combine our activities and do certain things for the salvation of men while we are in mortality, and then certain things are done for the salvation of men while they are in the spirit world awaiting the day of the resurrection.

Well, once again a revelation was given that affects this sphere of activity and the sphere that is to come. And so it has tremendous significance; the eternal import was such that it came in the way it did. The Lord could have sent messengers from the other side to deliver it, but he did not. He gave the revelation by the power of the Holy Ghost. Latter-day Saints have a complex: many of them desire to magnify and build upon what has occurred, and they delight to think of miraculous things. And maybe some of them would like to believe that the Lord himself was there, or that the Prophet Joseph Smith came to deliver the revelation, which was one of the possibilities. Well, these things did not happen. The stories that go around to the contrary are not factual or realistic or true, and you as teachers in the Church Educational System will be in a position to explain and to tell your students that this thing came by the power of the Holy Ghost, and that all the Brethren involved, the thirteen who were present, are independent personal witnesses of the truth and divinity of what occurred.

There is no way to describe in language what is involved. This cannot be done. You are familiar with Book of Mormon references where the account says that no tongue could tell and no pen could write what was involved in the experience and that it had to be felt by the power of the Spirit. This was one of those occasions. To carnal people who do not understand the operating of the Holy Spirit of God upon the souls of man, this may sound like gibberish or jargon or uncertainty or ambiguity; but to those who are enlightened by the power of the Spirit and who have themselves felt its power, it will have a ring of veracity and truth, and they will know of its verity. I cannot describe in words what happened; I can only say that it happened and that it can be known and understood only by the feeling that can come into the heart of man. You cannot describe a testimony to someone. No one can really know what a testimony is—the feeling and the joy and the rejoicing and the happiness that come into the heart of man when he gets one—except another person who has received a testimony. Some things can be known only by revelation. "The things of God knoweth no man, but the Spirit of God." (1 Corinthians 2:11.)

This is a brief explanation of what was involved in this new revelation. I think I can add that it is one of the signs of the times. It is something that had to occur before the Second Coming. It was something that was mandatory and imperative in order to enable us to fulfill all of the revelations that are involved, in order to spread the gospel in the way that the scriptures say it must spread before the Lord comes, in order for all of the blessings to come to all of the people, according to the promises. It is one of the signs of the times.

This revelation that came on the first day of June 1978 was reaffirmed by the spirit of inspiration one week later on June 8, when the Brethren approved the document that was to be announced to the world. And then it was reaffirmed the next day, on Friday, June 9, with all of the General Authorities present in the temple, that is, all who were available. All received the assurance and witness and confirmation by the power of the Spirit that what had occurred was the mind, the will, the intent, and the purpose of the Lord.

Well, this is a glorious day. This is a wondrous thing; the veil is thin. The Lord is not far distant from his church. He is not far removed.

President Kimball is a man of almost infinite spiritual capacity—a tremendous spiritual giant. The Lord has magnified him beyond any understanding or expression and has given him His mind and His will on a great number of vital matters that have altered the course of the past—one of which is the organization of the First Quorum of the Seventy. As you know, the Church is being guided and led by the power of the Holy Ghost, and the Lord's hand is in it. There is no question whatever about that. And we are doing the right thing where this matter is concerned.

There has been a tremendous feeling of gratitude and thanksgiving in the hearts of members of the Church everywhere, with isolated exceptions. There are individuals who are out of harmony on this and on plural marriage and on other doctrines, but for all general purposes there has been universal acceptance; and everyone who has been in tune with the Spirit has known that the Lord spoke, and that his mind and his purposes are being manifest to the course the Church is pursuing.

We talk about the scriptures being unfolded—read again the parable of the laborers in the vineyard (Matthew 20) and remind yourselves that those who labor through the heat of the day for twelve hours are going to be rewarded the same as those who came in at the third and sixth and the eleventh hours. Well, it's the eleventh hour; it's the Saturday night of time. In this eleventh hour the Lord has given the blessings of the gospel to the last group of laborers in the vineyard. And when he metes out his rewards, when he makes his payments, according to the accounts and the spiritual statements, he will give the penny to all, whether it is for one hour or twelve hours of work. All are alike unto God, black and white, bond and free, male and female.

STRENGTHENING THE FATHER IN THE HOME

President Ezra Taft Benson

In the priesthood, we are engaged in the greatest work in all the world: the building of men of character, men of strength and courage, men of deep spirituality, God-like men.

Each father in the Church is establishing, or should be establishing, his patriarchal order—an order that will extend into the eternities. As priesthood bearers and priesthood leaders, we have an opportunity to draw close to our brethren and help strengthen them in their priesthood duties.

The Lord has given us the broad outline of organization. He has set forth the objectives and purposes, but he leaves to us pretty much the working out of the methods. Here are some basic principles to guide us in this program of strengthening the fathers in their families.

1. *The home and family is the eternal unit and the basis of the righteous life.*

The home is the rock foundation, the cornerstone of civilization. The church, the school, and even the nation stand helpless before a weak and degraded home. No nation will rise above its homes, and no nation will long endure when the family unit is weakened or destroyed.

President David O. McKay wisely said, "No other success in life can compensate for failure in the home." If this nation is to endure, then the home must be safeguarded, strengthened, and restored to its rightful importance.

2. *The father is the presiding authority in the home. He is the patriarch or head of the family.*

President Harold B. Lee gave us the foundation for this principle when he stated: "The most important of the Lord's work that you will ever do will be the work that you do within the walls of your own home."

The worthy priesthood holder who magnifies both his priesthood and his fatherhood, who is a true patriarch in his family, may inherit great blessings, for the Lord has said:

"Ye shall come forth in the first resurrection; and if it be after the first resurrection, in the next resurrection; and shall inherit thrones, kingdoms, principalities, and powers, dominions, all heights and depths . . . and if ye abide in my covenant . . . it shall be done unto them in all things whatsoever my servant hath put upon them, in time, and through all eternity; and shall be of full force when they are out of this world; and they shall pass by the angels, and the gods, which are set there, to their exaltation and glory in all things, as hath been sealed upon their heads, which glory shall be a fulness and a continuation of the seeds forever and ever." (D&C 132:19.)

3. *The mother is the helpmate, the counselor.*

Through the Prophet Joseph Smith, the Lord said to Emma Smith, "Thou art an elect lady, whom I have called. . . . And the office of thy calling shall be for a comfort unto my servant, Joseph Smith, Jun., thy husband, in his afflictions, with consoling words, in the spirit of meekness. . . . Wherefore, lift up thy heart and rejoice, and cleave unto the covenants which thou hast made. . . . Keep my commandments continually, and a crown of righteousness thou shalt receive." (D&C 25:3, 5, 13, 15.)

In establishing this great patriarchal order, the mother must be considered a counselor, a close companion, in planning the execution of the program for the benefit and the blessing of the family.

4. *You cannot talk about father without talking about the role of the mother—they are one, sealed for time and all eternity.*

I make it a practice, whenever I perform a marriage, to suggest to the young couple that they return to the temple as soon as they can and go through the temple again as husband and wife. It isn't possible for them to understand fully the meaning of the holy endowment or the sealings with one trip through the temple, but as they repeat their visits to the temple, the beauty, the significance, and the importance of it all will be emphasized upon them. I have later had letters from some of these young couples expressing appreciation because that item was emphasized particularly. As they repeat their visits to the temple, their love for each other tends to increase and their marriage tends to be strengthened.

5. *The quorum is organized to teach, inspire, and strengthen the father in his responsibility and help him to do his duty.*

This suggests involvement—involving each priesthood holder in the programs of the Church, giving him something to do, assuring him that he is needed and wanted in the Church. Concerning our duty, the Lord has said: "Now let every man learn his duty, and to act in the office in which he is appointed, in all diligence. He that is slothful shall not be counted worthy to stand, and he that learns not his duty and shows himself not approved shall not be counted worthy to stand." (D&C 107:99-100.)

6. *If the father fails in his responsibility, the home teacher must work with him to strengthen and help him to do his duty.*

This involves, of course, a lot of person-to-person work and informal contacts. It also involves love for our fellowman and concern for him. "Let every man esteem his brother as himself." (D&C 38:25.)

"By this shall all men know that ye are my disciples, if ye have love one to another." (John 13:35.)

7. *The father has the responsibility for the physical, mental, social, and spiritual growth and development of himself, his wife, and each of his children.*

A young man once came to my office for a blessing. He had problems—not moral problems, but he was confused; he was concerned and worried. We talked for a few minutes and I said to him, "Have you ever asked your father for a blessing?" "Oh," he said, "I don't know that Dad would do a thing like that. He is not very active." I said, "But he's your father." "Yes." "Does he hold the priesthood?" "Yes, he is an inactive elder." "Do you love him?" And he said, "Yes, I love him. He is a good man, he's good to the family, good to the children." I said, "Do you ever have family prayer?" He said, "It has been a long time since we had family prayer." I said, "All right, would you be willing to go home and watch for an opportunity, and ask your father if he will give you a blessing? And if it doesn't work out, you come back and I will be glad to help you."

So he left, and in about three days he came back. "Brother Benson, this has been the sweetest thing that's happened in our home," he said. "Mother and the children sat there, my younger brothers and sisters, with my mother wiping the tears from her eyes. She expressed her gratitude later. Father gave me a lovely blessing." He added, "I could tell it came from his heart."

There are a lot of fathers who would enjoy giving their own children blessings, if they had a little encouragement. As patriarchs of their families, that is one of their obligations and duties, responsibilities, and, of course, opportunities.

8. *A father cannot be released from his responsibility.*

Bishops are called and serve for a while and then are released, but a father is never released. He may release himself through sin, but his is an eternal calling.

"I appeal to you parents, take nothing for granted about your children," said President J. Reuben Clark. "The great bulk of them, of course, are good, but some of us do not know when they begin to go away from the path of truth and righteousness. Be watchful every day and hour. Never relax your care, your solicitude. Rule kindly in the spirit of the priesthood, but rule, if you wish your children to follow the right path."

9. *A father has the responsibility to lead his family by—*

—loving God and looking to him for daily counsel and direction. That means he must have family prayer as well as personal prayer. I often wish there were some way to measure accurately the value of family prayer. What it would mean to little Mary, who is giving her first talk in Sunday School or perhaps her first little talk in Primary, to have the family go onto their knees that morning and make special mention of her that she will do her best and not be too frightened. What it would mean to a special teenage son who is facing a stiff examination in high school, to have him specially mentioned in family prayer. Family prayer can greatly increase the unity and solidarity in the family.

—loving his wife and being one with her. One of the

greatest things a man can do for his children is to love his wife and let them know that he loves her.

—desiring to have children and loving them. If he really loves them, he will want the home evening, he will want the family council, he will want them to be exposed to the programs of the Church.

—letting virtue garnish his thoughts unceasingly. This is one of the great needs today particularly. We have so much sin, so many men attracted by a pretty face, and untrue to their companions.

—being an example of all he wants to teach.

—teaching and training his children in the word of the Lord, in light and truth.

—teaching them repentance, faith in Christ, baptism, the gift of the Holy Ghost, enduring to the end, praying vocally and in secret. (See D&C 68.)

—governing, commanding, correcting, nurturing, and blessing them in meekness, tenderness, and love, and upon the principles of righteousness. (See D&C 121.)

—not provoking any family members so that they become discouraged.

—creating an environment in the home conducive to order, prayer, worshipping, learning, fasting, growth, happiness, and the Spirit of the Lord. I often like to refer to section 29 of the Doctrine and Covenants, where the Lord gives the assurance that Satan has no power over little children until they reach the age of eight; a father has the opportunity during those eight years, without interference from the adversary, so far as the child is concerned. I am grateful for that.

—dedicating his home to the Lord.

✳10. *The father must hunger and thirst and yearn to bless his family, go to the Lord, ponder the words of God, and live by the Spirit to know the mind and will of the Lord and what he must do to lead his family.*

It is soul-satisfying to know that God is mindful of us and ready to respond when we place our trust in him and do that which is right. There is no place for fear among men and women who place their trust in the Almighty, who do not hesitate to humble themselves in seeking divine guidance through prayer. Though persecutions arise, though reverses come, in prayer we can find reassurance, for God will speak peace to the soul. That peace, that spirit of serenity, is a great blessing.

Rearing eleven vigorous children to honorable manhood and womanhood on a small farm is no easy accomplishment. Yet, as my father and mother devoted themselves to this task, they never seemed to have any fear of the future. The reason was their faith—their confidence that they could always go to the Lord and he would see them through.

"Remember that whatever you do and wherever you are, you are never alone," was my father's familiar counsel. "Our Heavenly Father is always near. You can reach out and receive his aid through prayer."

All through my life the counsel to depend on prayer has been prized above any other advice I have ever received. It has become an integral part of me, an anchor, a constant source of strength.

11. *The Church exists to assist the father in getting his family back into the presence of our Father in heaven.*

Long after the Church has performed its mission, the celestial patriarchal order will still be functioning. This is why President Joseph F. Smith said, "To be a successful father or a successful mother is greater than to be a successful general or a successful statesman," and President David O. McKay added, "When one puts business or pleasure above his home, he, that moment, starts on the downgrade to soul weakness." And this is why President Harold B. Lee said, "The Church must do more to help the home carry out its divine mission."

Never has the devil been so well organized, and never in our day has he had so many powerful emissaries working for him. We must do everything in our power to strengthen and safeguard the home and the family.

The adversary knows "that the home is the first and most effective place for children to learn the lessons of life: truth, honor, virtue, self-control; the value of education, honest work, and the purpose and privilege of life. Nothing can take the place of home in rearing and teaching children, and no other success can compensate for failure in the home." (President David O. McKay, letter to parents in *Family Home Evening Manual*, 1968-69, p. iii.)

12. *Our pattern or model for fatherhood is our Heavenly Father.*

When Saul was on the road to Damascus, he was stopped by a heavenly vision and the voice of the Lord Jesus Christ. Saul responded with these momentous words: "Lord, what wilt thou have me to do?" (Acts 9:6.) To this the Lord responded by sending Saul to see one of his authorized servants to receive direction and a blessing.

A man can ask no greater question in his life than that which Paul asked: "Lord, what wilt thou have me to do?" A man can take no greater action than to pursue a course that will bring to him the answer to that question. The Lord has already suggested an answer to each of us when he said, "Be ye therefore perfect, even as your Father which is in heaven is perfect" (Matthew 5:46), and "Therefore, what manner of men ought ye to be? Verily, I say unto you, even as I am" (3 Nephi 27:27).

Christ, then, has set us the example of what we should be like and what we should do. While many men have admirable qualities, there is only one man who ever walked the earth who was without sin, and who had the power to resurrect his own body. This Jesus is our exemplar and has commanded us to follow in his steps. He is the way, the truth, and the light, and no one can come back into the presence of our Father in heaven except through him. That man is greatest who is most like Christ, and those who love him most will be most like him.

How, then, does a man imitate God, follow his steps, and walk as he walked? Through studying the life of Christ, learning his commandments, and doing them. God has promised that to follow this course will lead a man to an abundant life, a fulness of joy, and the peace and rest for which those who are heavy-burdened long. To learn of Christ necessitates the study of the scriptures and the testimonies of those who know him. We come to know him through prayer and the inspiration and revelation that God has promised to those who keep his commandments.

And how do we learn the commandments? Through the words of the Lord in the scriptures, through the revelations received by his authorized servants, through the Light of Christ, that inspiration which comes to every man, and through personal revelation by the Holy Ghost.

The family is under attack today as perhaps never before, and it is very real. Yet the family is the rock foundation, the cornerstone of civilization. The Church will never be stronger than its families. Home teachers, quorum leaders, all of us, need to get the father to recognize his great responsibility to perform his duty as a father and as a patriarch to his own children.

At a stake presidency's meeting in Boise, Idaho, years ago, we were trying to select a president for the weakest and smallest elders quorum in the stake. Our clerk had brought a list of all the elders of that quorum, and on the list was the name of a man whom I had known for some years. He came from a strong Latter-day Saint family, but he wasn't doing much in the Church. If the bishop made a call to do some work on the chapel he'd usually respond, and if the elders wanted to play softball, you would sometimes find him out playing with them. He did have leadership ability; he was president of one of the local service clubs and was doing a fine job.

I said to the stake president, "Would you authorize me to go out and meet this man and challenge him to square his life with the standards of the Church and take the leadership of his quorum? I know there is some hazard in it, but he has the ability."

The stake president said, "You go ahead, and the Lord bless you."

After Sunday School I went to the man's home. I'll never forget the look on his face as he opened the door and saw a member of his stake presidency standing there. He hesitantly invited me in; his wife was preparing dinner, and I could smell the aroma of coffee coming from the kitchen. I asked him to have his wife join us, and when we were seated, I told him why I had come. "I'm not going to ask you for your answer today," I told him. "All I want you to do is to promise me that you will think about it, pray about it, think about it in terms of what it will mean to your family, and then I'll be back to see you next week. If you decide not to accept, we'll go on loving you."

The next Sunday, as soon as he opened the door I saw that there had been a change. He was glad to see me, and he quickly invited me in and called to his wife to join us. He said, "Brother Benson, we have done as you said. We've thought about it and we've decided to accept the call. If you brethren have that much confidence in me, I'm willing to square my life with the standards of the Church, a thing I should have done long ago." He also said, "I haven't had any coffee since you were here last week, and I'm not going to have any more."

He was set apart as elders quorum president, and attendance in his quorum began going up—and it kept going up. He went out, put his arm around the inactive elders, and brought them in. A few months later I moved from the stake.

Years passed, and one day on Temple Square in Salt Lake City, a man came up to me, extended his hand, and said, "Brother Benson, you don't remember me, do you?"

"Yes, I do," I said, "but I don't remember your name."

He said, "Do you remember coming to the house of a delinquent elder in Boise seven years ago?" And then, of course, it all came back to me. He said, "Brother Benson, I'll never live long enough to thank you for coming to my home that Sunday afternoon. I am now a bishop. I used to think I was happy, but I didn't know what real happiness was."

When we bring the fathers back into activity, we bring them happiness in this life, to say nothing about the eternal blessings that are opened up to them. My heart goes out to those men, heads of families, who are inactive, prospective elders. I don't believe we have a greater challenge in the Church today than to activate those men and bring them to the point where they can take their families to the house of the Lord and have opened to them the richest blessings known to men and women in this world, and closely related to the blessings in the world to come.

WOMEN AND
THE PRIESTHOOD

Elder Robert L. Backman

It was my great privilege to perform the temple sealing ceremony for a fine young couple. Following the ceremony, a wedding breakfast was held to honor them. Because the bridegroom was a member of the ward in which we lived, my wife and I were invited to attend. Following the meal, a short program had been arranged in which the sweet bride was to sing to us. When her turn came, she stood in front of us, smiled with adoration at her new husband, and began to sing these lovely sentiments from Ruth 1:16:

"Intreat me not to leave thee, or to return from following after thee: for whither thou goest, I will go; and where thou lodgest, I will lodge."

That was as far as she could go before she choked and started to cry. Soon she was sobbing so hard she could not continue. She stood before us unable to control her emotions. Finally, when she regained her composure, she apologized for her tears, then exclaimed, "I never knew I could be so happy!"

Considering the transcendent importance of the temple sealing she had experienced, the bride's tears of joy were well shed, for she had been a covenanting party, with her husband, to that sacred ordinance which literally opened the door to exaltation and eternal life for them, dependent only on their faithfulness.

As I share similar experiences with other young couples in the house of the Lord, I often wonder whether they appreciate that sealing ceremony and the saving ordinances that precede it; whether they understand their unique roles as man and woman—his patriarchal leadership and her matriarchal duties, his priesthood responsibilities and her sustaining obligation. In the first blush of romance, too few consider the eternal consequences of their marriage or the necessity of planning for the delicate balance they will need in their relationship if there is to develop a celestial marriage, that is, a marriage sealed by the Holy Spirit of Promise.

In this day of discontent when there is such a crusade for "equality" among the feminists, men and women seem to be more in competition with than complementary to each other as God intended they should be. Leah D. Widtsoe told the story of the small brother and sister who were competitively discussing their future: "The boy stated he could be an engineer when he grew up and drive a huge engine. The girl said she could be a great musician and thrill great audiences with the joy of her art. The boy retorted that he could be President of the United States. For a while the little girl was somewhat silenced for surely here her brother had the better of the argument. Suddenly a bright thought came. 'When I grow up I can be a mother and have a baby all my own and nurse it!' That seemed to silence the lad until this bright thought came, 'but I can hold the priesthood!' " ("Priesthood and Womanhood," *Relief Society Magazine*, October 1933, p. 598.)

Unknowingly, those two children distinguished the unique roles of man and woman that led the Lord to declare: "Nevertheless neither is the man without the woman, neither the woman without the man, in the Lord." (1 Corinthians 11:11.)

God has decreed that man may hold the priesthood and woman may become a mother, and thus they are dependent upon each other. Neither can achieve exaltation and eternal life without the other. Although the Lord has not revealed to us the secrets of our sexual origin, he has disclosed that "man was also in the beginning with God. Intelligence, or the light of truth, was not created or made, neither indeed can be." (D&C 93:29.)

That passage would lead us to believe that we have always been what we are now, man or woman. Our roles as man or woman were fixed even before we were created. John A. Widtsoe wrote: "A wiser power than any on earth understands why a spirit in the far off beginning was male or female." (*Priesthood and Church Government*, Deseret Book, 1950, p. 90.)

From the account of the creation of the earth, we learn that "God created man in his own image, in the image of God created he him; male and female created he them." (Genesis 1:27.)

Since we chose to come to this earth to gain bodies and enjoy earth's experiences, we must have known of our individual roles and consequences of our being man or woman. Yet we "shouted for joy" at the opportunity.

The account of Adam and Eve in the garden is the basis for understanding our roles as man and woman. Because Eve was the first to eat of the forbidden fruit, the Lord said: "I will greatly multiply thy sorrow and thy conception. In sorrow* thou shalt bring forth children, and thy desire shall be to thy husband, and he shall rule over thee." To Adam he declared: "Cursed shall be the ground for thy sake; in sorrow shalt thou eat of it all the days of thy life. . . . By the sweat of thy face shalt thou eat bread." (Moses 4:22-23, 25.)

Dr. Hugh W. Nibley emphasizes the similarity of the curse upon Adam and Eve in these words:

"If Eve must labor to bring forth, so too must Adam labor (Genesis 3:17; Moses 4:23) to quicken the earth so it shall bring forth. Both of them bring forth life with sweat and tears, and Adam is not the favored party. If his labor is not as severe as hers, it is more protracted. For Eve's life will be spared long after her childbearing—'nevertheless thy life shall be spared'—while Adam's toil must go on to the end of his days. 'In sorrow shalt thou eat of it *all* the days of thy life!' Even retirement is no escape from that sorrow. The thing to notice is that Adam is not let off lightly as a privileged character; he is as bound to Mother Earth as Eve is to the law of her husband. And why not? If he was willing to follow her, he was also willing to suffer with her, for this affliction was imposed on Adam expressly 'because thou hast hearkened

---

*Dr. Hugh W. Nibley has suggested that the true meaning of "sorrow" in these verses is "not to be sorry, but to have a hard time." Considering the joy attendant to having a family or in doing satisfying work, his translation becomes very meaningful.

unto thy wife and hast partaken of the fruit.' " ("Patriarchy and Matriarchy," *Blueprints for Living: Perspectives for Latter-day Saint Women*, Brigham Young University Press, 1980, p. 46.)

They were partners and rejoiced in their respective roles, for they knew they were dependent upon each other: Adam to till the ground, support the family, give righteous leadership; Eve to sustain him, bear the children, and rear them in truth. The scriptures tell us that they blessed the name of God, and Eve was glad; otherwise they never would have had seed (Moses 5:11), nor could they have had joy in this life or eternal life hereafter.

God ordained that man should hold the priesthood. He presides in the home; he blesses his wife and family; he leads in righteousness; he is the patriarch. It is through the exercise of the power of his priesthood and the ordinances thereof that he and his wife may be sanctified and the family unit projected beyond the grave.

God is a God of order. He knows that leadership is necessary in all our relationships to avoid chaos. Since man has the responsibility of priesthood, his must be the final voice to preserve family integrity. His is the power of presidency. God is no respecter of persons. He is just and treats all with equality. He expects that the man who bears the priesthood and the woman who honors the priesthood will provide joint leadership in the home through love and mutual understanding. When used in the spirit of persuasion, long-suffering, gentleness, meekness, and love unfeigned, by kindness and pure knowledge (see D&C 121:41-42), the priesthood unites men and women, for it is the power of salvation, the only power by which we can return to the presence of God. It is only in the ordinances of the priesthood that we can attain eternal life and exaltation.

When God decreed that the husband should "rule over" the wife, he did not give him dictatorial power. As with all the powers of the priesthood, this power must be exercised righteously. The wife is to obey the laws of her husband only as he obeys the laws of God. In his forthright manner, Brigham Young declared: "I have counseled every woman of this church to let her husband be her file leader; he leads her and those above him in the Priesthood lead him. But I never counseled a woman to follow her husband to hell." (Quoted in *Relief Society Magazine*, November 1933, p. 669.) He also said, "Let the husband and father learn to bend his will to the will of his God, and then instruct . . . in this lesson of self-government by his example as well as by precept." (*Discourses of Brigham Young*, Deseret Book, 1954, p. 198.)

Dr. Nibley reminds us that "the gospel sets absolute limitations beyond which patriarchal authority may not be exercised—the least hint of unkindness acts as a circuit-breaker, 'Amen to the priesthood or authority of that man.' (D&C 121:37.)" (*Blueprints for Living*, p. 50.) In those homes where fathers and sons exercise their priesthood in righteousness and where mothers and daughters honor and sustain them in that exercise, we are likely to find families progressing through life with a true understanding that families are eternal.

Although a woman does not receive, hold, or exercise the power of the priesthood independent of her husband, she certainly shares its eternal blessings. She is the immediate beneficiary of many of its blessings when she is married to a priesthood bearer in the house of the Lord, for the blessings pronounced on their heads are of equal importance to both husband and wife and are to be realized only as both partners honor the covenants they have made at the holy altar. Exaltation cannot be realized by either one alone.

President and Sister Spencer W. Kimball serve as powerful examples of this eternal partnership. Sister Kimball has stated: "Marriage is an equal partnership between husband and wife. Each has a specific role. The man fills most successfully the role of director and protector. His position, hopefully, is never carried out autocratically but in perfect love and with cooperative consideration.

"The woman is to acquire the attributes of love and patience, unselfishness and endurance. She should be skilled in child training, economics and management, nutrition and nursing. Anyone who would say apologetically, 'I am only a homemaker' has not fully appreciated the importance and intricacy of her profession.

"In the home, the woman should teach her children to honor and respect their father, who should properly preside and lovingly direct the activities of the family." (BYU Today, December 1980, p. 4.)

When man and woman are in perfect balance in their relationship, each is the glory of the other. Woman is not inferior to man. She has unique physical and spiritual gifts and powers. As a husband and father, I recognize more every day how much my wife is the heart of our marriage. A woman is expected to develop her talents, school her intellect, exercise her gifts, and progress and grow spiritually, mentally, socially, and morally. She has her free agency. She is on the path of eternal progression. President Kimball has said about Sister Kimball: "Camilla is a most delightful and brilliant companion, a wonderful mother and grandmother, an excellent leader in the Church, and a wonderful neighbor. She is an educated woman, both intellectually and spiritually, and this has made her a significant woman and, frankly, an interesting person to be with." (BYU Today, December 1980, p. 4.)

There is no limit to a woman's development, for it is her destiny to become a queen and a priestess, and to inherit the fulness of the glory of God.

Yet the question remains, why should God give his sons a power that is denied his daughters?

In a general conference speech, Elder William J. Critchlow, Jr., asked: "Did women by their own first choice choose to be partners with God in his creative processes? Faced with an alternative—partnership or priesthood—did you, Sister, pass up priesthood? Did women by their own free choice choose to be the family heart rather than the family head?" (Improvement Era, December 1965, p. 1120.)

Walking by faith, we do not know the answer to that question. We do know that, by virtue of the fall, Eve was to submit to her husband and she was to bear children. That responsibility is borne solely by the woman. It is a most sacred calling in carrying out God's plans for his children. Granted the blessing of motherhood, woman was given the most God-like of all life's experiences and can thereby appreciate, more than any man, the intensity of the suffering of our Savior.

This was so beautifully expressed by President J. Reuben Clark:

"From that day, when Eve thus placed first among her blessings the power to bear children, the greatest glory of true womanhood has been motherhood.

"What a miracle is motherhood; how nearly infinite is mother. She fashions in her womb the most complex structure known to man, the whole visible universe being, in contrast, the simplest of creations. From the cell she herself has built from the dust of the earth, fructified by the father cell formed also of dust of the earth by the father, she mounts cell on cell, each born of clay, till the normal man is brought into the world . . . a body fashioned in the very image of the Son who was in the image of the Father. What an infinitely glorious concept, what a supreme destiny, and what a divine-like achievement.

"This is wife's and mother's task and opportunity and did she fail so that new body-forms came or that none came, then the Great Plan would fail and God's purposes would come to naught. They must build in the likeness of the Father and the Son. This must never change." ("Our Wives and Our Mothers in the Eternal Plan," *Relief Society Magazine*, December 1946, p. 801.)

I stand in awe of motherhood and the sublime love it represents. Two examples will illustrate the singular relationship between mother and child.

I sat in a courtroom hearing a man sentenced to death for murder. He stood before the judge, defiant and unrepentant, as those fateful words were pronounced. Then, as the guards placed handcuffs on him to return to prison, I witnessed a touching scene. A small woman approached the condemned man, threw her arms around him, kissed him on the cheek, and whispered to him that she loved him. It was his mother, who, through her own sorrow and anguish, distinguished the criminal from the crime and reached out to comfort him who was despised because of his heinous crime. Her love was as Christ-like as anything I have seen.

The other example involved my own beloved daughter. She faced the delivery of her baby by an emergency cesarean section, and because her husband was away, she invited me to be with her to bless and sustain her during the operation. I blessed her by the power of the priesthood, then accompanied her to the delivery room. She was given a spinal block and was fully conscious as the surgeons performed that delicate procedure. I sat beside her, holding her hand, kissing her beautiful face, and offering what comfort I could. I was amazed to note how calm she was. We discussed the absolute miracle in the conception, development, and birth of a baby and wondered what adventures the child would have in life. We heard the first faint cries of the baby as he was removed from the warmth and security of his mother's body. I saw the tears of joy, the sublime smile, and the blessed relief that were evident on my sweetheart's countenance when she knew the baby was here, alive, and healthy. The baby's cries grew louder as he was bathed and wrapped in a towel. A nurse placed that tiny infant in my arms, and I held him as my daughter checked him over to be certain he was all there. The protesting cries from that little soul grew stronger and stronger until I placed his little face next to the cheek of his mother. Then, instantaneously, he stopped crying, comforted by the knowledge that he was next to his own flesh and blood, to that one person who would go to the edge of death to bring him life. I was so grateful for that experience, which gave me some insight into the eternal bond that is the singular relationship between mother and child.

Are women inferior to men? If women understood the full scope of their power to shape the future of the world, there would be danger of their having a superiority complex, for there is no greater power on earth than motherhood! Knowledge of its full scope and possibility should make women feel neither inferior nor superior, but truly humble and willing to learn that they may exercise that power unceasingly for the improvement and blessing of all mankind.

"When the real history of mankind is fully disclosed, will it feature the echoes of gunfire or the shaping sound of lullabies? The great armistices made by military men or the peacemaking of women in homes and in neighborhoods? Will what happened in cradles and kitchens prove to be more controlling than what happens in congresses? When the surf of the centuries has made the great pyramids so much sand, the everlasting family will still be standing, because it is a celestial institution, formed outside telestial time. The women of God know this." (Neal A. Maxwell, *Ensign*, May 1978, pp. 10-11.)

The wise woman will place her motherhood above every claim and not allow it to become secondary to anything.

What of those good women who do not have the opportunity to marry in this life, who have no husband with whom they can share the blessings of the priesthood? God, being a just God, will not deny them any of the blessings of the faithful. Joseph Fielding Smith gave this counsel to our single women:

"You good sisters, who are single and alone, do not fear, do not feel that blessings are going to be withheld from you. You are not under any obligation or necessity of accepting some proposal that comes to you which is distasteful for fear you will come under condemnation. If in your hearts you feel that the gospel is true, and would under proper conditions receive these ordinances and sealing blessings in the temple of the Lord; and that is your faith and your hope and your desire, and that does not come to you now; the Lord will make it up, and you shall be blessed—for *no blessing shall be withheld.*" (*Doctrines of Salvation*, Bookcraft, 1955, 2:76.)

In the meantime, dear sisters, your lives may be blessed through the priesthood of your fathers, brothers, sons, bishops, and home teachers. Take every opportunity the gospel affords you to become acquainted with your Father in heaven and his divine plan for his children. And remember always that he loves you.

Finally, these are the words of John Taylor as he described the destiny of the faithful woman who has married in the house of the Lord, honored her husband, borne and reared her children in righteousness, developed her own gifts and talents, and served her fellowmen throughout her life. Not only will her joy be full and her reward great on earth, but the glory of God will be hers hereafter:

"Now, crowns, thrones, exaltations and dominions are in reserve for thee in the eternal worlds, and the way is opened for thee to return back into the presence of thy Heavenly Father, if thou wilt only abide by and walk in a celestial law, fulfil the designs of thy creation, and hold out to the end. That when mortality is laid in the tomb, you may go down to your grave in peace, arise in glory, and receive your everlasting reward in the resurrection of the just, along with thy Head and husband. Thou wilt be permitted to pass by the Gods and angels who guard the gates, and onward, upward to thy exaltation in a celestial world among the Gods. To be a *priestess queen* unto thy Heavenly Father, and a glory to thy husband and offspring, to bear the souls of men, to people other worlds, (as thou didst bear their tabernacles in mortality,) while eternity goes and eternity comes; and if you will receive it, lady, this is eternal life. And herein is the saying of the apostle Paul fulfilled, 'that the man is not without the woman, neither the woman without the man, in the Lord.' (1 Cor. 11:11.) 'That man is the head of the woman, and the glory of the man is the woman.' (1 Cor. 11:7.) Hence, thine origin, the object of thy creation, and thy ultimate destiny, if faithful. Lady, the cup is within thy reach; drink then the heavenly draught, and live." (*The Mormon*, August 29, 1857.)

THE GREATEST
BROTHERHOOD

President N. Eldon Tanner

For the past few years I have been associated with an organization known as the National Conference of Christians and Jews. This is a national organization with councils in cities all across the country, manned by local officers and committees. In Salt Lake City, a Catholic, a Protestant, a Jew, and a Mormon all work together as co-chairmen in the interest of promoting fellowship and brotherhood. I have thought what a wonderful thing it would be to extend this kind of fellowship to all religions and people throughout the world.

The president of this organization, Dr. David Hyatt, has stated: "Brotherhood—the respect for the dignity and worth of another human being—must become a part of our conscious activities, not just philosophical rhetoric or afterthought. . . . Brotherhood is democracy at work! It is giving to others the rights and respect we want for ourselves. It can be that simple and that profound!" ("We Need You to Combat Intergroup Bigotry and Prejudice," NCCJ pamphlet, December 1974, p. 3.)

As I have observed the members of this organization and have studied their aims and ideals, I have been impressed with what I have seen them accomplish through people working together in harmony and in unity to achieve their purposes. As I have thought of this and other groups working for brotherhood or sisterhood, or to promote other causes or projects, my mind has always come back to the organization of the priesthood of God, which is the greatest and most important brotherhood association in all the world. How fortunate we are to be members of it!

But with that membership comes great responsibility as well as great opportunity. It is not enough for us to be members and to be satisfied with the numbers we have in our respective quorums. We want to reach out and embrace all the world in our brotherhood, which is the only organization designed to bring them the greatest gift they could receive—eternal life!

Latter-day Saints are in a unique position because they know and understand that all human beings are literally the spirit children of God, and the family unit is eternal and can enjoy eternal progression, which should be the goal of all. Because we know that God is our Father, we refer to one another as brothers and sisters, just as children in families do, and we enjoy a true feeling of brotherhood.

Some people ask the reason for an organized church. They feel they can work out their salvation alone, and that there is no need to attend church meetings or fill other requirements so long as they are honest and honorable and do good to their fellowmen. But the Lord has given us instructions that we should belong to a church; and this, his church, has the same organization that Jesus Christ himself established while he was on the earth. We have many explicit declarations from the Lord that make this clear, and that also tell us that we need to encourage and help one another.

He said: "And that thou mayest more fully keep thyself unspotted from the world, thou shalt go to the house of prayer and offer up thy sacraments upon my holy day." (D&C 59:9.)

Another: "It is expedient that the church meet together often to partake of bread and wine in the remembrance of the Lord Jesus." (D&C 20:75.)

Further, he said: "And I give unto you a commandment that you shall teach one another the doctrine of the kingdom." (D&C 88:77.)

And he admonished: "When thou art converted, strengthen thy brethren." (Luke 22:32.)

All of these instructions are to help us enjoy life here and prepare ourselves to go back into the presence of our Heavenly Father. For this purpose the earth was created, and we find a scriptural account setting forth God's plan for us: "We will go down, for there is space there, and we will take of these materials, and we will make an earth whereon these may dwell; And we will prove them herewith, to see if they will do all things whatsoever the Lord their God shall command them." (Abraham 3:24-25.)

To accomplish God's purposes and to prove ourselves, it is necessary that we work within his church and under the direction of his authorized servants. We need the strength that comes from association with others who are seeking the same goals.

To illustrate this, I should like to repeat a story related by Elder Henry D. Taylor a few years ago in a talk which he gave at general conference and which he entitled "Man Does Not Stand Alone."

"A boy was extended an invitation to visit his uncle who was a lumberjack up in the Northwest. . . . [As he arrived] his uncle met him at the depot, and as the two pursued their way to the lumber camp, the boy was impressed by the enormous size of the trees on every hand. There was a gigantic tree which he observed standing all alone on the top of a small hill. The boy, full of awe, called out excitedly, 'Uncle George, look at that big tree! It will make a lot of good lumber, won't it?'

"Uncle George slowly shook his head, then replied, 'No, son, that tree will not make a lot of good lumber. It might make a *lot* of lumber but not a lot of *good* lumber. When a tree grows off by itself, too many branches grow on it. Those branches produce knots when the tree is cut into lumber. The best lumber comes from trees that grow together in groves. The trees also grow taller and straighter when they grow together.' "

Then Brother Taylor made this observation: "It is so with people. We become better individuals, more useful timber when we grow together rather than alone." (*Conference Report*, April 1965, pp. 54-55.)

Elder Sterling W. Sill, in an article entitled "Men in Step," wrote: "The greatest invention of all time is said to have taken place 2500 years ago at Platea when an obscure Greek perfected the process of marching men in step. When it was found that the efforts of a large group of people having different motives and different personalities could be organized and coordinated to function as one, that day civilization began." ("Insights & Perspectives," March 1977, from *Leadership*, Bookcraft, 1958, 1:222-29.)

When all priesthood holders of the Church are in step to march as the army of God in doing our duty, helping one another, looking after the Church, fellowshipping all mankind, then we will be accomplishing God's purposes and doing what he intended for us to do when he established his church.

The Church has established the welfare program through which we can work in an organized way to assist those who are in need. Men and women spend countless hours working together in welfare projects, which will be stocked against the time of need therefor by persons other than themselves. What a great feeling it is to realize that all throughout the Church we have facilities for producing and dispensing commodities that have been placed in storehouses ready to be distributed to the needy among us.

This is true brotherhood in action—to labor or support financially programs for persons one may never see or hear about. It is easy to do things for our own families and loved ones, but to give of our substance for the stranger who is in need is the real test of our charity and love for our fellowmen.

Another area where we work for the benefit and blessing of some we do not know is in the field of our temple and genealogical work. We perform thousands and thousands of ordinances for those who have died without having had opportunity to do for themselves those things which are necessary for their advancement in the kingdom of heaven.

In both these areas of our church activity it is inspirational to see groups of men and women working side by side in good fellowship to accomplish something for somebody else. These projects strengthen personal relations between those who are working together and build testimonies of the truthfulness of a gospel that teaches that we are our brother's keepers, and "inasmuch as ye have done it unto one of the least of these my brethren, ye have done it unto me." (Matthew 25:40.)

Sometimes we can get inactive brethren involved in

such projects; and when they catch the spirit of the work, they will want to continue their association with their brethren in quorum meetings. President David O. McKay once said: "There are many ways in which we can get these indifferent elders together without inviting them to do things which are difficult. Some of them do not like to pray. They hesitate about standing in public to preach, and some of them would rather go fishing or playing golf on Sunday than attend meeting. But, not one of those indifferent elders will refuse an invitation, for example, to come to a funeral of one of the townsfolk, or one of their members, or of one of their members' wives, and if you will come as a quorum and sit together as a quorum, there is one means of fellowship." (*Conference Report,* October 1951, p. 179.)

In this same train of thought, President McKay said on another occasion, addressing the members of the priesthood: "Fellow presiding officers in missions, stakes, wards, and quorums, *make your quorums more effective in regard to brotherhood and service.* The quorums are units which should effectively hold the priesthood in sacred bonds and in helpfulness.

"I refer particularly to the senior members of the Aaronic Priesthood—you businessmen, successful in the business world; you professional men who have devoted your time to the success of your vocations and are successful and are leading men in civic and political affairs—get together more closely in your quorum . . . and help one another. If one of your number be sick, two or three of you get together and call on him. . . .

"You elders perhaps have one of your number sick, and his crop needs harvesting. Get together and harvest it. One of your members has a son on a mission, and his funds are getting low. Just ask if you can be of help to him. Your thoughtfulness he will never forget. Such acts as these are what the Savior had in mind when he said, 'Inasmuch as ye do it unto the least of these my brethren, ye do it unto me.' (See Matt. 25:40.)" (*Conference Report,* October 1955, p. 129.)

In order to extend this brotherhood to all the world, we send out thousands of missionaries in keeping with the Savior's injunction to "go ye therefore, and teach all nations, baptizing them in the name of the Father, and of the Son, and of the Holy Ghost: Teaching them to observe all things whatsoever I have commanded you: and, lo, I am with you alway, even unto the end of the world." (Matthew 28:19-20.)

It is always interesting to hear returned missionaries, no matter where they have labored, say they served in the greatest mission in the world. This is because they have caught the spirit of missionary work and become persuaded that all men are brothers and children of God. As they teach the gospel, they learn to replace with love any prejudice they might have felt for the people among whom they labor. It is remarkable what the Spirit of the Lord can do for us.

We pray every day that governments of countries which are now closed to our missionaries will open their gates to make it possible for us to teach them the gospel, which alone will bring full understanding of the fatherhood of God and the brotherhood of man. We want to explain how they can return to live with God, their Father, and be reunited with their families, and eventually live eternally as one great family.

Though we are accused of prejudice, there is no people any place in the world with greater love for, and interest in, humanity than the Latter-day Saints. We express this feeling of brotherhood through the principles we teach and the work we do. We have mentioned temple work for the dead, our welfare services, and the great missionary program. We also express our concern and interest in our fellows through the home teachers of the priesthood organizations and the visiting teachers of the Relief Society. Where these visits are made as they should be, members of the Church should feel that they are fellowshipped into a great brotherhood or sisterhood.

For the past few years I have had the privilege of home teaching with an ordained teacher part of the time, and a priest with whom I am teaching at the present time. They make the appointments and take their turn in presenting and leading the discussions. The other day my home teaching companion called me and said that the head of one of the families we visit was in the hospital and suggested that we go to see him. We did and blessed him.

I relate two other experiences to demonstrate what I mean. One of our Church members was transferred to New York City to direct the work of a Church-owned radio station. He had never been to New York before, but he located one of our chapels and attended church the first Sunday he was there. He was welcomed into the priesthood quorum as a brother, and his wife and children were similarly welcomed and were soon right at home.

In contrast, at the same time another young man whom he knew was sent by his company to operate another station. Though he was a member of a church that had many times the membership of our church, he found it most difficult to feel at home and soon asked for a transfer back to his original station. It might have been his fault, or it might have been the fault of his church. However, in our church, if the individual and the quorum are functioning as they should, all members should feel happy, wanted, and accepted wherever they go.

Another experience was related to me by a priesthood holder. This is what he said:

"I, with my wife and teenage son and daughter, had a very serious car accident. My wife, daughter, and son escaped without any serious injury. The car was totaled. As I was pulled out of the wreck, I was in a state of shock, paralyzed, and semiconscious. The wreckers could not figure out how we came out alive.

"As people came to the scene of the accident, one man ordered them not to move me for fear of causing paralysis. He was the first man on the scene, and as he examined me he found that I was wearing temple garments. He was a Mormon. After seeing me safely in the ambulance and on the way to the next town, he alerted the bishopric; and as I arrived at the hospital the brethren were there to administer to me. The attending physician at the hospital was a stake president.

"For the next week I was on the critical list, and a

member of the bishopric insisted that my wife and family stay at his home, taking meals and shelter there. After three or four days my wife and family returned home to Phoenix, and the members of the ward rallied around my family to help wherever they could. One good brother offered the use of his private plane or motor home to bring me back home. We used the motor home, which made it possible for them to slide the stretcher into it.

"When I arrived home there were many friends there to greet me, and my dear friend and member of my priesthood quorum who is a fine physician took care of me. We cannot express our gratitude to those who offered assistance in so many ways, but most definitely we witnessed there the priesthood in action and always will be grateful to be members of The Church of Jesus Christ of Latter-day Saints where such brotherhood is fostered."

President Stephen L Richards, a former counselor in the First Presidency, said: "I have reached the conclusion in my own mind that no man, however great his intellectual attainments, however vast and far-reaching his service may be, arrives at the full measure of his sonship and the manhood the Lord intended him to have, without the investiture of the Holy Priesthood, and with that appreciation, my brethren, I have given thanks to the Lord all my life for this marvelous blessing which has come to me—a blessing that some of my progenitors had, and a blessing which more than any other heritage I want my sons and my grandsons and my great-grandsons to enjoy." (*Conference Report*, October 1955, p. 88.)

I pray that it might be truly said of us, "Well done, thou good and faithful servant." (Matthew 25:21.) May we assist our prophet in accomplishing his great desires for the benefit and blessing of all mankind. His primary and most worthy goals are to take the gospel to every nation, kindred, tongue, and people, and to build temples wherein the work can be done to seal on earth and in heaven those blessings reserved for the faithful righteous. May we strive with all our hearts, minds, and strength to do what the Lord would have us do in preparation for his second coming. I fully believe that when he comes he will call on the faithful brethren who hold his priesthood in preference to any others to assist him in the consummation of his glorious work. I know he lives, that he will come again; and it is my earnest prayer that we will be worthy to meet him and assist him.

INDEX

Index

Calling and election made sure, blessing of priesthood, 34-45
Callings: do not diminish quorum membership status, 91-92; are appendages to priesthood, 91-92
Car accident, family in, fellowshipped, 163-64
Celestial marriage: blessing of priesthood, 32-33; must be sealed through Holy Spirit of Promise, 111-12; seriousness of, 147-48
Children, rearing of, 54
Christlike life, defined, 53
Church: transition in government of, 56-57; to help father exalt family, 143-44
Clark, J. Reuben, on priesthood government, 15
Confessions are confidential, 69-70
Council of Twelve: filling vacancies in, 39-40; governed Church after ascension of Savior, 40; call of first, in last dispensation, 42-44; charge to, by Oliver Cowdery, 44-45
Couples should return to temple often, 139-40
Courtship, thoughtfulness in, 5
Cowdery, Oliver: description of Aaronic Priesthood restoration, 14-15; charge to Council of Twelve, 44-45

Deacons, duties of, 81-82
Decisions, making, to be righteous, 5-6
Desire, in magnifying callings, 16-18
Disciples carried apostolic ministry in America, 41
Discipline: an expression of love, 90-91; comes from word *disciple*, 91
Divorce, Brethren concerned about, 4-5

Durham, G. Homer, chapter by, 23-29

Elements, power to govern, blessing of priesthood, 33
Elijah held priesthood keys, 25
Eternal life, power to gain, blessing of priesthood, 33-34

False priesthood on earth with true priesthood, 11
Family, basis of righteous life, 138
Family prayer, blessings of, 141
Father: presides in home, 138-39; eternal blessings of, 139; must be sealed to mother, 139-40; responsible for development of family members, 140-41; gives reluctant son blessing, 140-41; cannot be released, 141; duties of, 141-42; to seek inspiration for family, 142-43; should emulate God, 144-45; inactive, called to lead quorum, 145-46
Fathers, the, 1-2
Featherstone, Vaughn J., chapter by, 101-12
Fyans, J. Thomas, chapter by, 117-25

Genealogy work, 60-61
Gentiles, discussion over whether, should obey law of Moses, 40
Goals, priesthood holders should set, 5
God, seeing face of, blessing of priesthood, 35
God, sons of, to become, is blessing of priesthood, 32
Gospel: is blessing of priesthood, 30-31; goes to various peoples on priority basis, 129-31; to go to all nations before Second Coming, 131